The Creative Journal for Children

≪ ≪ ≪ ≪ ≫ ≫ ≫ ≫

The Creative Journal for Children

A GUIDE FOR PARENTS, TEACHERS, AND COUNSELORS

≪ ≪ ≪ ≪ ≪ ≫ ≫ ≫ ≫ ≫

Lucia Capacchione

FOREWORD BY GERALD G. JAMPOLSKY, M.D.

SHAMBHALA

Boston & London

1989

SHAMBHALA PUBLICATIONS, INC.
Horticultural Hall
300 Massachusetts Avenue
Boston, Massachusetts 02115
www.shambhala.com

For information about Lucia Capacchione's books, lectures, workshops,
and trainings, contact:
  Lucia Capacchione
  P.O. Box 1355
  Cambria, CA 93428
  (310) 281-7495

15   14   13   12   11   10

Printed in Canada
⊗ This edition is printed on acid-free paper that meets the American
National Standards Institute Z39.48 Standard.

Distributed in the United States by Random House, Inc., and in Canada
by Random House of Canada Ltd

Library of Congress Cataloging-in-Publication Data

Capacchione, Lucia.
The creative journal for children.

1. English language—Composition and exercises—
Study and teaching (Elementary)   2. Diaries—Authorship.
3. Self-perception in children.   4. Creative ability in
children.   I. Title.
LB1576.C316   1989   372.6'23   89-42621
ISBN 0-87773-497-6

Dedicated to child diarist Anne Frank, whose life has touched so many and whose heart and words burned with a flame that neither prison nor death could extinguish.

Contents

≪ ≪ ≪ ≪ ≫ ≫ ≫ ≫

Foreword

≪ ≪ ≪ ≪ ≫ ≫ ≫ ≫

In our work at the Center for Attitudinal Healing we are aware of how important it is to create an environment in which children can feel safe and unthreatened about sharing their innermost thoughts and feelings. One way our children express their thoughts and feelings about catastrophic illness is through drawing and writing, and many of their drawings have been shared through the book they wrote collectively, *There Is a Rainbow Behind Every Dark Cloud.*

Lucia Capacchione's *Creative Journal for Children* also provides a safe environment for children to, as she describes it, "find the buried treasure within: feelings, experiences, intuition, and dreams." Since grades and criticism are not a part of her journal method, and sharing is voluntary and therefore unthreatening, children can relax and enjoy using this journal as a vehicle for self-exploration and self-expression.

From her experience as an educator and art therapist she has found that when children speak from the creative self and are encouraged to say what they really want to say, basic educational skills can be acquired much more easily and naturally. I agree with Lucia when she says, "Our jobs as parents, teachers, and counselors become a true joy when we can be quiet long enough to let the children speak from within." *The Creative Journal for Children* encourages children to do just that, and as a result, we adults find out who the real teachers are.

Gerald G. Jampolsky, M.D.
Founder of the Center for Attitudinal Healing
Author of *Love Is Letting Go of Fear*

Preface

≪ ≪ ≪ ≪ ≫ ≫ ≫ ≫

This book is intended as a practical guide for parents, counselors, and teachers wishing to guide children in journal-keeping. It contains basic principles and techniques and is fully illustrated with examples from children's journals.

These exercises are designed for use with very young children (preschool and kindergarten) as well as elementary and junior high school youngsters. The youngest contributor was two and a half; the oldest was fifteen. Since mental and emotional maturity can differ greatly, I have not attempted to establish the appropriateness of the exercises according to chronological age. Rather, I have left it up to the parent, counselor, or teacher to select the exercises most appropriate for the child or children involved. I have included suggestions about situations in which the exercises may be most fruitful as well as variations for children who cannot read or write.

For best results, I recommend that you first use my book for adults, *The Creative Journal: The Art of Finding Yourself* (Athens, Ohio: Ohio University/Swallow Press, 1979, 1988). Keep a journal of your own, and experience the method for yourself. The best teacher of journal-keeping is a journal-keeper.

Acknowledgments

≪ ≪ ≪ ≪ ≫ ≫ ≫ ≫

My appreciation goes to all the educators, parents, and counselors who have supported the Creative Journal Method by using it with children. Love and special thanks to:

Dr. Raymond Terrell and Dr. Randall Lindsay, School of Education, California State University at Los Angeles, whose encouragement and support enabled me to introduce this method into the public schools.

Roberta Curinga for her enthusiastic guidance as director of our pilot project in the Garvey School District in Rosemead, California.

Elizabeth Johnson for her assistance in field-testing and gathering illustrations for this book.

Dr. Gerry McCormack, who introduced the Creative Journal to the Lawndale School District and the staff of Mark Twain Elementary School for their creative application in the classroom.

Zena Schaffer and the staff of Farmdale Elementary School, Los Angeles Unified Schools, for integrating this method into their curriculum.

Jean Katz for her heart-felt encouragement and the opportunity to train special education teachers in the Los Angeles County Schools.

Lura Jane Geiger and Adam Geiger of LuraMedia in San Diego for believing in this work and helping me get it into the hands of those who needed it.

My early teachers—Sister Mary Ceciliana, John Otterson, Sister Mary Corita—for seeing the best in me and for helping me express it.

Dr. Maria Montessori, whose work inspired me to enter the teaching profession and whose spiritual message—that learning unfolds from within—has continued to illuminate my life.

Anaïs Nin for introducing me to the magic world of the diary.

All the children who have been my teachers by touching my heart with their pictures and words.

My associates, Nancy Shaw and Jim Strohecker, for their continued support.

My editors at Shambhala Publications, Emily Hilburn Sell and Kendra Crossen.

My daughters, Celia Pearce, for her invaluable assistance in the initial phases of developing this material, and Aleta Pearce, for her encouragement and support in word processing and preparing the text for publication.

My father, for encouraging me to become a writer when I grew up.

My mother, for giving me my first diary and supporting me in cultivating all my talents in the arts.

The contributors to this book: Crista Barnes, age 2 1/2; Noelle Barnes, age 9; Tony Fino, age 6; Hiram Henriques, age 7; Wendi Lee, age 12; Carmen Melendez, age 12; Celia Pearce, age 15; Michael Rice, age 7; Isa Rosenbloom, age 8; Daniel Sutphin, age 7; Daniel Weismann, age 11; and David Weismann, age 9.

A Note to Grown-ups

≪ ≪ ≪ ≪ ≫ ≫ ≫ ≫

Dear Grown-ups:

Please don't use this book like a "schoolbook" to be forced onto young people. It will do them good because it will help them know and love themselves better. That is the best reason for using it.

Please don't tell them, "Do this because it's good for you. I know best."

Trust that children can and do want to find *for themselves* what's best for them.

So offer this book and this work with love and respect for the wisdom of the children and young people. No matter what you do, with that attitude, you will help them and yourself.

With love,
Lucia Capacchione

ONE

The Creative Journal Method

≪ ≪ ≪ ≪ ≪ ≫ ≫ ≫ ≫ ≫

When I was a little girl, my mother had a book that always fascinated me. It was bound in brown alligator skin, it had gold edging on the pages, and the word DIARY was embossed in gold on the cover. There was a leather flap from the back cover to the front that kept the book secured shut with a shiny gold lock. My mother never locked her diary, however, for she never wrote in it. There were no secrets there, only a tiny gold key in a little paper envelope. There were no words in it except for a year's worth of dates printed in chronological order on the neatly lined pages.

I didn't know why, but I loved that little empty diary. Maybe it was the antique appearance that appealed to me. I liked to feel the bumpy leather binding, to look at the richness of the gold edging on the pages and the shininess of the tiny lock and key. The book was so fancy that I couldn't imagine anyone actually writing in it. Also, there was something wonderful and mysterious about the blankness of the book. It was full of possibilities.

Then one day I was given a diary of my own, bound in plain royal blue imitation leather. It wasn't as fancy as my mother's, so I felt okay about writing in it. It was like my mother's in every other way, though, right down to the flap, the lock and key, and the word DIARY in gold on the cover. I was delighted with it.

At first, it was fun. Faithfully, I made an entry each day. "Dear Diary, Today (so and such happened) and then . . ." And so it went. But after a while, I felt cramped by the small space provided for each day's entry. There was so much to say and so little room. Later, boredom set in. The fun of chronicling events wore thin, and gradually I stopped writing to my Dear Diary altogether.

The writing didn't stop, however. At school, I wrote well and with great enthusiasm. My teachers were very encouraging. I had talent, they said. Later, while recovering from pneumonia, I discovered a talent for art. I filled sketch pads with drawings of people, nature, and objects. Again the teachers encouraged me to develop my artistic abilities.

I kept a steno pad in my closet, and every now and then I would dig it out and write about something important to me: my teacher at art school, the artists I admired, my own paintings. I loved doing this kind of writing so much that I'm surprised I did it so infrequently.

When I was fifteen, I won second prize in an essay contest sponsored by our local newspaper. The theme was "future career," and I wrote about how I'd been inspired to become a journalist someday. While collecting my prizes from a local store, I bought a little black and red, hardbound ledger-type book with the word RECORD neatly embossed in gold on the cover. The pages were blank except for lines. Buying the book was a special treat. I reasoned that since I was going to be a journalist, I would need a very special notebook in which to write. Perhaps I'd even write a book, I thought.

But I put the book away and promptly forgot all about it and about becoming a journalist. I became an artist instead. Later on, I became a parent and a teacher. The years passed.

Then, during a serious illness when I was thirty-five, I found the little record book I'd purchased twenty years earlier. I sat in my sickbed and wrote out my deepest feelings and thoughts, pain and fear, wishes and dreams, the words of my inner world. This was my first "official" journal. And the process of journal-keeping, first through writing and then through a blend of pictures and words, helped me heal myself from a mysterious illness that had defied the doctors and their medication.

After my recovery I changed careers and became a counselor specializing in art therapy and a method of journal-keeping based on my experiences. I taught courses for adults and wrote a handbook called *The Creative Journal: The Art of Finding Yourself.*

In looking back I see that, at fifteen, I had no way of consciously knowing where that little record book would lead me. How could I have known that I would carry it around among my possessions for twenty years before writing a word in it? How could I have known that instead of being a journalist's notebook, it would become the first volume in a continuing series of personal journals?

Yet at age fifteen, I intuitively knew that little record book was very special. I'm sure that's why I kept it all those years. For on the day I bought it, a dream was set in motion. Even though it went underground for twenty years, that dream and the book that symbolized it were there when I needed them most. My girlhood dream came true, although not in the form I had expected. I became a "journalist" after all, a journalist of the inner life. And I'm grateful to that fifteen-year-old girl that I was for having the sense to buy a little blank book. I used it to save my life.

WHAT IS CREATIVE JOURNAL-KEEPING?

Creative journal-keeping is a tool for gaining self-understanding and practicing language skills through writing and drawing. It consists of simple exercises to be done in a diary or personal journal. The Creative Journal Method nurtures self-esteem while strengthening communication skills. It develops imagination and creative abilities as well as concentration and clarity.

This volume of Creative Journal techniques is intended for use with children from kindergarten through junior high school.

The exercises are designed to help children:

- express feelings and thoughts
- feel comfortable drawing and writing
- acquire the habit of self-reflection and self-expression
- learn to communicate experience in words and pictures
- become more observant of themselves and others
- foster a positive self-concept
- exercise imagination and innate talent
- strengthen attention span and ability to focus
- enrich language and art skills through regular practice
- develop a greater sense of self-responsibility
- use both visual and verbal processes (right and left brain)
- find resources and wisdom within

The exercises are arranged in sequence from simple to more complex, from concrete experiences to imaginative visualization. The table of contents lists the exercises by name so you can easily locate the ones you wish to use. Once you have studied the material, however, you may want to present the exercises in another order. I encourage you to do whatever feels right. *You* know the children you are working with. *You* can respond to their changing needs and to their cues as to which exercise is appropriate at the time. Once they've started their journals and are familiar with this approach, the children can choose exercises for themselves or make up their own.

In using the Creative Journal Method, I hope you will approach it as a tool. Consider it an open-ended springboard, an enhancement of your educational or counseling goals or both. It is a means of stimulating language and self-communication—be innovative and playful with it:

- Modify or expand the exercises.
- Use journal activities from other sources (see Suggested Readings, pages 22–23).
- Invent new journal techniques, or ask the children to do so.

TALENT AND CREATIVITY: WE'VE ALL GOT IT

When children begin journal-keeping, some of them are hesitant to draw, just as adults are. You may hear comments such as "I can't draw" or a lot of nervous giggling. This is more common with older children of school age. The very young (kindergarteners and preschoolers) have not yet learned that they "can't draw," for these are learned attitudes—make no mistake about it.

All human beings are potentially creative and expressive. Unfortunately, in our culture most people think they are untalented or uncreative in art or writing or both. How many times have you heard, or even said, "I can't draw a straight line," or "I'm just not artistic," or "I don't have any talent"?

These learned beliefs usually stem from criticism of early attempts at self-expression. Fear of further ridicule and failure easily leads to the conclusion that you lack talent: a wonderful excuse for not developing abilities. First, you buy the idea that you don't have "it." And if you don't have "it," then you can't possibly use "it." Right? Wrong! It is just this kind of distorted logic based on a mistaken belief that blocks creative growth in any area of activity.

The truth is that people can't draw because they *think* they can't and because they never *do* it. It's as simple as that. They were educated with little or no encouragement, training, or opportunity in art. In the case of writing, they may have received formal instruction, but it was always attached to grades and judgment. Writing is rarely approached as an inherently fulfilling activity, something to be done for one's own pleasure and self-expression.

That's where the Creative Journal comes in. It's a safe place to test the waters of self-expression. It's confidential, so no one is going to see it and possibly ridicule or disapprove of it. It's not being critiqued or graded, like other school assignments. The only "critics" the journal-keeper has to deal with are the ones inside: the negative beliefs that cause feelings of self-doubt, inferiority, awkwardness, stupidity, lack of talent, and so forth.

If you are willing to encourage journal-keeping and protect the children's right to privacy, you can help them unlearn their feelings of inferiority about writing and drawing. Experience shows that children who start out by saying, "I can't," eventually relax into drawing and writing if the pressure to perform has been removed from the atmosphere.

As one elementary school teacher said, after several months of journal work with her class, "My kids *never* say they can't draw anymore. They're too busy *doing* it."

In fact, it is common for children to develop a fond attachment and feelings of pride and ownership about their journals. Many teachers have told me how upset their students are if a journal-keeping period is missed. Others report that some of the kids hold their journals very dear and are distraught if they can't find them. "They even clutch them to their little hearts," one teacher said. Another one said, "It's as if the journal is some sort of mother." I think this is an accurate image. The journal is a place to nurture what is best within the self, and I think children understand that. While I was writing this book I was invited to train elementary teachers in the Garvey School District in Rosemead, California. All of the children in the two pilot schools kept journals. One little girl wrote:

> Dear Journal:
>
> Today is my first time I had you. I think your a nice Journal to be with. I hope to have you for ever and ever. I'm going to tell you lots of things about me. I like you a lot and I thank the people that gave us the money to get you. . . .

THE VALUE OF JOURNAL-KEEPING FOR CHILDREN

SAFETY

The journal is a safe place for children to express themselves because it is private and confidential. It provides practice in communication free from judgment, ridicule, or failure.

RELAXATION

Children can relax with their journals and get their thoughts and feelings out on paper without having to analyze or edit the work.

SPONTANEITY

Since it is not being done for performance or external scrutiny, journal work encourages honest expression and spontaneity. This opens up the child's innate intuition and creativity.

INTEGRITY

The privacy of the journal fosters integrity and honesty with oneself. Since it is not intended for others to see, the child is communicating with him- or herself. This is like looking in a mirror.

EXPERIMENTATION

The absence of pressure to perform or compete with others makes the journal a safe place to experiment with written language and art and to discover things that haven't been said or done before. This is a key element in the creative process. Since the pages of the journal are blank, whatever emerges is of the child's own making.

COMMUNICATION

Journal-keeping reinforces communication skills through the habit of drawing and writing about personal experiences, feelings, and thoughts. It is an excellent supplement to a language arts curriculum and can easily be integrated into the instructional program. It also provides practice in child-made books, in which children write and illustrate their own stories and poems.

ORAL LANGUAGE

Both the drawn and written journal exercises foster spoken expression. This may begin with dictation about the drawings (for preschoolers and nonreaders) and then develop into written journal work. The voluntary sharing that accompanies journal work also aids in oral language development.

GATHERING IDEAS

The journal is an excellent place to record creative ideas and make notes for use in developing more formal "public" writing, such as classroom assignments, letters, and essays.

IMAGINATION

The integration of drawing and writing in the Creative Journal Method stimulates imagination, creativity, and originality. It fosters a respect for innovation, brainstorming, and applying new ideas.

CREATIVITY

The Creative Journal activities develop creative abilities in art and writing as well as other areas because they foster observation and self-expression.

VERBAL AND NONVERBAL EXPRESSION

Using both art and writing makes the Creative Journal helpful for less verbal children (nonreaders and nonwriters) as well as those with language skills. It is especially effective with children who are noncommunicative, emotionally disturbed, or learning disabled.

RIGHT BRAIN DEVELOPMENT

Journal exercises in drawing stimulate visual thinking and perceiving ("right brain" processes), which are often ignored in traditional modes of instruction. This is crucial for children whose learning or cognitive style is characteristically nonverbal.

LEFT BRAIN DEVELOPMENT

Regular writing in the journal encourages verbal ("left brain") development. The sequential nature of verbal thinking is introduced in the beginning with the very nature of the page-by-page, day-at-a-time entries in the journal of the prereader. As words are dictated and then written by the child, he or she masters comprehension and expression through regular practice.

INTEGRATION

The integration of drawing and writing stimulates both visual and verbal thinking, both right and left brain development. It also leads to balanced learning and communicating. Rational and intuitive processes are given equal time and attention. Innovation and structure flourish side by side.

EMOTIONAL RELEASE

Because of its confidential nature, the journal provides an unthreatening place to release feelings and pent-up emotions that may not have other outlets. The encouragement the child receives for expressing feelings in the journal fosters an acceptance of those feelings and of the self.

SELF-UNDERSTANDING

Spontaneous drawing and reflective writing make Creative Journal exercises excellent tools for learning about oneself. The honesty and spontaneity that are encouraged set the stage for gaining insight into personal experience.

AUTOBIOGRAPHY

The personal nature of the journal makes it a perfect vehicle for developing autobiographical sketches and writing. In fact, the autobiographies of many famous people are simply collections of diary or journal writings.

SELF-CONFIDENCE

The nonjudgmental quality of journal-keeping helps build the self-esteem and self-confidence necessary for developing creative abilities and an attitude of success in life. One of the most common reports from parents and teachers is that journal-keeping raises self-esteem in children, and the confidence that this develops carries over into all areas of life.

VALUES CLARIFICATION

The self-reflective nature of creative journal-keeping provides children with excellent tools for exploring their own personal values, preferences, desires, and talents.

USES OF CREATIVE JOURNAL-KEEPING

Children can benefit from journal-keeping in a great variety of situations—at home, at school, in hospitals, or while traveling.

IN TIMES OF TROUBLE

Journal work is especially useful during times of crisis or major changes, such as the following:

- family crisis
- moving
- changing schools, classes, or grades
- addition of a new family member
- death of a loved one
- divorce or separation
- illness or injury
- conflict with others.

These events are often accompanied by difficult feelings such as: physical or emotional pain, confusion, anger, fear, and grief.

At such times, the journal can be a good friend, a place to express all the feelings inside. Sometimes it is hard for children to express difficult feelings in words, so drawing can be a perfect form of expression. At other times the words are there, but there is no person to tell them to. So the journal "listens" and "takes it all in"—without judgment, without blame. The diaries of Anne Frank and Anaïs Nin demonstrate the great benefits of having someone to confide in when no one else is there (that "someone" being the self).

AT HOME

Oftentimes children are at loose ends during summer vacation and weekends or while convalescing from an illness or injury. During these unstructured periods, children complain about not having anything to do. This is especially true in bad weather or when they are alone. Out of sheer boredom and frustration, children often turn to habitual television-watching simply because they can't think of anything better to do. They become addicted passive consumers of other people's imaginative (or not-so-imaginative) creations.

Journal-keeping can be a refreshing alternative to adult manufactured entertainment. Unlike television, journal-keeping requires *active* participation and personal involvement. The journal page is like a blank television screen, with the *child* creating the picture or words on the screen out of his or her own experience and imagination. Journal-keeping encourages thinking and communicating, stimulates creativity, and fosters emotional awareness and expression. It can provide an important at-home reinforcement of learning skills taught at school, especially in subjects that rely on language and verbal communication. It can also be the vehicle for types of expression that are not being developed in the school curriculum, such as drawing, poetry, and autobiographical writing about personal or family values and culture.

WHILE TRAVELING

A journal makes a wonderful traveling companion. Journal-keeping is an excellent way to record experiences on short trips and vacations. Children often become restless when spending long hours in cramped quarters such as cars, buses, trains, or planes. Drawing and writing in a journal can help them use their time productively and can enrich the journey. There are always novel experiences on trips: new people and places, unfamiliar sights and sounds, a wide variety of feelings. All of these provide wonderful raw material for creative expression. Like a photo album, a travel journal is a record of memories that can provide happy reminiscences for years afterward.

AS AN ADJUNCT TO COUNSELING OR THERAPY

Dream journals have long been used as an integral part of psychoanalysis, especially in the Jungian tradition. The Creative Journal Method provides a new tool, a beautiful complement to any form of psychological therapy or family counseling. The exercises can be suggested for homework, or they can actually be done during the counseling session.

During my years as an art therapist I used journal activities with my clients. Since the publication of my first book, *The Creative Journal,* many professionals in the mental health field have used these techniques successfully. Some professionals have received training from me; others have simply used my book and told me of their experiences. These include:

- art therapists and poetry therapists
- movement therapists and play therapists
- marriage, family, and child counselors
- physicians
- nurses

Professionals tell me that journal work and journal sharing seem to intensify the therapy process, helping them and their clients gain deeper insights. Many counselors actually use the exercises in therapy sessions, as I did. They find that this approach is particularly effective with less verbal individuals, who are greatly helped by drawing and other visual forms of expression.

Professionals are especially grateful for the journal as follow-up or independent homework. This is probably the most important aspect of journal-keeping: *it develops the individual's sense of personal responsibility, self-reliance, and self-respect.* What could be more therapeutic than that? Feelings and dreams, thoughts and experiences can be expressed when they're fresh, instead of being stored up or "put on ice" until the next counseling session. Often, in the very act of drawing and writing a feeling or dream, the individual resolves whatever was troubling him or her and no further interpretation is needed. There are many such examples in my books. They speak for themselves.

Journal-keeping is also valuable for self-maintenance, when formal therapy has been terminated. Many of my former clients express their gratitude for this "self-therapy" tool that has become such a valuable resource in times of stress. As one girl said, "It's wonderful knowing I have my journal to turn to whenever I need it. It's always there. And I can have it for the rest of my life." Of course, what she's really saying is that she has herself to turn to; she can rely on her own inner resources.

IN HOSPITALS AND OTHER TREATMENT CENTERS

I discovered journal work while struggling with a serious and mysterious illness. I have no doubt whatsoever that keeping a journal was the major factor in my healing.

At the Center for Attitudinal Healing in Tiburon, California, Dr. Gerald Jampolsky has pioneered some similar approaches to healing, which I can only describe as miracle-minded. By sharing their experiences and feelings about their life-threatening illnesses, children and their families are helping others facing similar catastrophes. A significant part of Jampolsky's work is the use of imagery and active imagination, including writing down and drawing personal experiences.

Jampolsky collected the writings and drawings of the children in the Center's program in a book entitled *There Is a Rainbow Behind Every Dark Cloud*. I know of no better example of journal-type activities for sharing and healing the body-mind. I urge you to read and use the "Rainbow" book as a companion to the Creative Journal, even if you are not working with children who are ill. If you work in a hospital or treatment clinic, or if you have a child of your own who is ill or handicapped, Jampolsky's book is a must.

The healing that comes with expressing emotions and experiences accompanying serious illness cannot be overemphasized. The exercise in Chapter 2, "My Body, Myself," is designed with this in mind. It has helped many people of all ages to deal effectively with physical symptoms, illness, and even chronic conditions. Children are especially good at using healing techniques, such as this one, that rely on the use of imagination and visual imagery. Drs. Carl and Stephanie Simonton have worked with children who have healed themselves by assigning symbolic pictures to an illness such as leukemia and creating an imaginary "drama" in which the "good guys" (health) wins out. The Simontons' methods appear in their book *Getting Well Again*.

As a treatment modality, the journal is well suited for use with bedridden children. During a period of illness it is easy to escape into watching television. Journal-keeping is a valuable antidote to such escape. It helps the child exercise the mind and the imagination even if the body must remain still. In the case of an injury to the dominant (writing) hand or side of the body, I recommend that the child use the nondominant hand (the one not normally used for writing).

IN SCHOOLS AND EDUCATION PROGRAMS

The applications of creative journal-keeping to education are virtually unlimited. Any subject matter, any theme can be explored in a journal through drawing or writing. The advantage of journal work is that it draws upon the student's own experience of the subject or concept being taught. It makes learning more concrete, personal, and alive. And it is free of the grades and negative judgment that often cause blocks and resistance to learning.

My adult journal students who were parents or teachers began using my method in a modified form with their own children at home or with their young students at school. These adults were highly enthusiastic about the results they saw: increase in language skills, greater ease of communication, improvement in handling and expressing difficult emotions, increased interest in drawing and writing for pleasure, and increased self-motivation and self-esteem.

As more and more parents and teachers urged me to develop exercises suited to young children, a golden opportunity to field-test these methods presented itself at the Garvey School District in Rosemead, California. As the Arts Team Coordinator for a federally funded project, I included journal-keeping in the curriculum for the program "Basic Skills Using Arts and Computer Personalization." Journals were given to every child in two pilot schools, Marshall Elementary (K–6) and Fern Avenue (K–3).

The feedback from administrators and teachers in these pilot programs was very positive. Of all the activities in the arts curriculum, the journal seemed to be the most successful. It was easily implemented, consistently used, and popular with the children. It worked in group-oriented instructional settings as well as in child-centered open classrooms. It worked with English-speaking children as well as those for whom English was a second language. These school populations consisted mostly of Asian-American and Latino children, many of whom speak no English when they enter school. Reading and math scores showed a twenty-percentile-point gain in one year in many of these classrooms.

BEHAVIOR PROBLEMS

Sometimes the journal is used to help children with behavior problems. One fifth-grader who was having trouble was asked to write her feelings down in her journal. After a page or so of venting anger, she decided she was tired of being mad and decided to "get off it."

LEARNING DISABILITIES

Journal-keeping can be very effective with children who have learning disabilities. It provides pressure-free practice in language and thought and develops a habit of organizing and communicating experience in visual and verbal forms.

CREATIVE BLOCKS

The Creative Journal aids children who have psychological blocks about art or writing. It offers a setting in which they can get over their self-consciousness about the *products* of their expression and can enjoy the *process* of drawing or writing. After some experience with this unthreatening form of communication, the children stop saying they can't draw or write, and they learn to enjoy both media.

The applications are unlimited, so I encourage you to use your own creativity in finding new uses. The list beginning on page 5 will give you further ideas on how to apply this method with your own children or with your students, patients, or clients. For several reasons, I'd very much like to hear from you about new approaches to this material. First, I'd like to expand my own understanding of its usefulness. Second, I often get requests for information on how journal-keeping can be used in various settings such as hospitals, detention homes, orphanages, special education schools, and counseling clinics. I would like to be able to create a network of people with similar interests and experience in pioneering new applications to journal-keeping with children. You can write to me at P.O. Box 5805, Santa Monica, CA 90405.

GENERAL GUIDELINES FOR JOURNAL-KEEPING

EXERCISE FORMAT

This book contains a series of journal exercises, each with its own descriptive name, procedure, purpose, and suggested uses. There is a *how, why,* and *when* for each activity presented.

Read the exercises over before reading or explaining them to the child. Become familiar with the format and the themes as well as the purposes and applications. This will help you to be more effective in your use of this material.

You will notice that the procedure section (*how*) is often divided into subsections. Give the exercise one subsection at a time, otherwise the child is likely to become overwhelmed and confused by too much information. Some of these exercises are too lengthy for one short journal session, so they'll need to be spread out over a couple of sessions or more.

I recommend that you use the following procedure:

1. Give the exercise name and instructions in the first part of the exercise.
2. Allow time for the child to do that part of the exercise. Use your own judgment about how much time will be needed so that you don't interrupt the child in midexercise.
3. When the child has completed the first part of the exercise, continue (if there are other parts and if there is time). Give

the next subsection and repeat the procedure outlined above until the exercise is completed. This may all be done on the same day, on consecutive days, or in later journal sessions.

PRESENTATION

The journal exercises can be read or told in your own words, if you wish. Give the exercises as suggestions: *never force or coerce a child*. That defeats the purpose of journal-keeping.

If you work with children who read, after they've grown accustomed to journal-keeping you can type the exercises onto 3″ × 5″ cards for them to use. Leave out the parent/teacher information (*why* and *when*) and simply put down the exercise title and the procedure (*how*).

After presenting the exercise, allow for questions, so that any confusion or misunderstanding can be discussed and cleared up before the work is begun.

Allow at least ten minutes for any subsection of an exercise. Some exercises take much longer and each child has individual time needs. Be aware of all of these variables when you plan a journal session or presentation.

Remember that the goal of these exercises is to motivate and inspire creative expression and self-understanding. The notes in each exercise on *why* and *when* will help you select exercises that are appropriate to your children's needs, skills, and interests. You may have to modify and adapt the activities to your own setting and requirements. I strongly advise you to do so. The more creative you are in using this book, the more you will enjoy it and the more the children will benefit.

SETTING

Journal work is best done in a quiet setting. If done at home, a comfortable and private place is best, one that is free from interruptions and distractions. In a classroom, children can work at their desks. A quiet, library-like atmosphere is important. It is helpful to establish a period of silent relaxation or reflection before journal work is begun.

TIME

Doing journal work *regularly* is a good way to acquire the habit and the skill. It need not be done every day, but the more often the journal is used, especially in the beginning, the more benefits it will yield.

For children who want to keep a journal at home, a ten- to thirty-minute session is recommended. If the child wants to do it on a regular basis, it is helpful to establish a consistent time, such as early morning or bedtime. The child should choose the time. Even if a regular time has been established, be aware that feelings or thoughts come to the surface and want expression at any time.

IN SCHOOLS

Many teachers report that they allot ten to fifteen minutes each day or three times a week for journal work. Others allow as much as thirty minutes per journal session a couple of times a week. Some teachers of reading, writing, English, ESL, creative writing, and art use journals in the context of their course work. They might give a short journal exercise on a particular experience of the subject. Or a journal assignment might be given for homework as reinforcement and integration of a new skill or concept.

SPONTANEITY

Encourage the child to use the exercise as a springboard in order to spark creativity and free expression. These exercises are not sacred. If the child improvises or changes an exercise, that is all to the good. We do not want to limit children but simply to help them open the door into themselves and their ability to communicate.

PRIVACY

Children's journals must be personal, private, and confidential, and children should be told this right from the start. They should know that they need never share anything from their journals if they don't want to. This cannot be overemphasized: *children should not be forced to share their journals.*

In order to maintain privacy, suggest that children keep journals in their own "safe" place such as a desk (at home or at school), cabinet, closet, special carrying bag, or the like. Some teachers who do journal-keeping with their students keep the journals in a locked cabinet in the classroom so that they won't get lost, stolen, forgotten, or damaged at home. The children take the journals out during "journal time" every day, or at other regularly designated times, but they return them to their special place.

At Santa Fe High School in Whittier, California, journals were used in a writing program. A journal club was established and privacy was maintained through a system of numbering the journals and keeping a confidential record of student numbers and names. Since the student names did not appear on the journals, their identity was protected in case of loss or theft.

In a home setting, the parent or guide and the child can discuss the best place to keep the journal. They can also establish family ground rules of respect for journal privacy.

Children can be *invited* to share from their journals, but only *if they wish*. Their unwillingness to share *must be respected at all times*. This is very important. Children should know that journal work is for themselves, not to get grades or approval from others. This is one place where the pressure of performing for others is removed. If and when children feel safe to share their journal work, they will. If not, leave them alone.

Some children will share with one other child or a trusted adult but not a group. Other children feel fine about reading from their journals or showing their drawings to an entire classroom. The *same* child may prefer one-to-one sharing on one day, group sharing on another day, or no sharing on still another day. In the classroom, journal pals can team up in pairs or groups to share journal work if they wish. Use your own discretion.

MATERIALS FOR JOURNAL-KEEPING

1. *Notebook with sturdy binding, 8-1/2" × 11" or 6" × 9"*
Each child has his or her own notebook. The best is a hardbound blank book with unlined white paper, 8-1/2" × 11", available at art supply and stationery stores. This is the best size for both writing and drawing. Spiral-bound sketch pads or notebooks with unlined paper can also be used.

An inexpensive journal can be produced in quantity in schools by having plain white paper bound in plastic comb binding. Most school districts now have comb binding machines. A heavier-weight, cover stock colored paper can be used for the front and back covers. This type of blank book can also be made up in copy shops for parents or counselors wishing to do journal work with children.

2. *Colored felt pens or crayons for drawing; pens or pencils for writing*
A set of eight colored felt pens is recommended for drawing. Any size marker is acceptable, although a medium or thin point that can be used for writing and drawing is most versatile. A pen or pencil can be used if colored pens are not available. In classrooms, children often share drawing tools such as crayons and felt pens. Eight colors or more should be provided.

PREPARING TO GUIDE CHILDREN'S JOURNAL-KEEPING

1. Present the idea of journal-keeping to the child or children. Discuss the points mentioned in the section on "The Value of Journal-Keeping," page 5.

If you are a journal-keeper, share your own experiences and give examples of the benefits you've received.

Find out how much the child or children know about journals and diaries. Have they ever kept one? Do they know anyone else who has? Cite Anne Frank's *Diary of a Young Girl* as an example of a child's journal that was published and became famous (it even became a play and then a movie). Read excerpts from it to the children. If the children are old enough, suggest that they read Anne's diary themselves.

If a regular schedule of journal-keeping is to be followed, establish it at this time (daily, three times a week, etc.).

2. Present the blank book or notebook to the child or children. Include the drawing and writing tools.

3. Explain that you will suggest things to draw or write about but that each child is also free to make up journal themes or topics on his or her own time.

4. Tell the children about the privacy of the journal and determine how privacy can be maintained during journal work times and when storing the journals. Discuss the voluntary option of journal-sharing and be sure the children understand this. *It is very important that children feel safe about their journal work and know they will not be coerced to share.* If privacy can't be guaranteed, the child or children may decide not to keep a personal journal. They have that right.

5. Talk about the importance of a quiet setting and the library-like atmosphere recommended for journal work. In discussion with the children, encourage them to share ideas for how to establish the appropriate environment.

6. Explain that each day's journal entries will be dated on the first page only. For nonreaders/nonwriters, put the date on the page for the children. For children learning to write, give them a "model" of the date to copy into their own journals. This can be done on the chalk board or on a card.

7. In the beginning it is best for the adult to assign the exercises. If you are working with older children, later on you can let them choose exercises for themselves. At home or in an open classroom, you can type or print some exercises on 3″ × 5″ cards so that each child can select which exercises he or she wants on that particular day. The goal is eventually to give the children as much choice and autonomy as possible. This way they will learn to trust their own inner guidance in finding what is right for them. Eventually children will be able to create their own exercises or simply write and draw

spontaneously. Even when they've achieved that degree of independence, it's advisable to use structured exercises for stimulation, inspiration, and focus.

8. Before doing journal work, ask the children to sit quietly with their eyes closed to shut out distractions and to go "inside" themselves. Find out if they have ever meditated or if they understand the concept of "going inside" and being quiet with themselves. Ask them to sit silently with you, eyes closed, for a few minutes so that they can experience "quiet time" in preparation for journal work. It is especially important that you model a calm manner and tone of voice to establish a relaxed atmosphere.

9. Ask the children to open their eyes and to remain silent. All the journal-keeping materials should be ready and at hand. Be sure to have the children date the journal page.

10. Read a journal exercise aloud. If there is a time limit, tell the children how much time is scheduled for the journal work and sharing time. *Make sure* they understand the *voluntary* nature of sharing. *No less than ten minutes* should be allotted for journal work. Fifteen to twenty minutes is preferable and, for some exercises, thirty minutes would be more appropriate.

STRUCTURING JOURNAL WORK IN THE CLASSROOM

GATHERING TOGETHER

In group instruction, if a special journal time is scheduled, I recommend the following. Begin with a quiet gathering together. It is preferable to sit in a circle with the students. If this is not practical, then simply have everyone come to silence at their desks.

SHARING

If students have been doing journal work at school or at home on their own, you may provide time here for sharing anything they want to share on their own. They may share an actual journal exercise/entry or their reaction to doing it. They may want to share something that happened in their lives in relation to doing the journal work.

QUIET TIME

Ask students to close their eyes and be in silence. Have them shut out external distractions and go inside. The best way to lead this "quiet time" is to speak in a calm voice and pause for a few minutes. Setting a tranquil atmosphere is very conducive to doing creative, introspective journal work.

Ask the students to open their eyes and remain silent. Read the journal exercise you have selected.

If there are any questions about how to do the exercise, this is the time for students to ask—while the group is still together and quiet.

If the students are in a circle, have them go to their own desks or to some "private" place in the room where they can work without interruptions or distractions. Establish a library-like atmosphere of quiet. *This is very important.* If the students are already sitting at their desks, go on to the next step.

Depending on the exercise and your time schedule, allow ten or more minutes for the students to do the journal exercise you have assigned.

Sharing can be done in many ways, as follows:

One-to-one partners

Students can team up in pairs and quietly share anything they want to about the exercise they just did. You can suggest that partner A share for a few minutes, with partner B listening. Then reverse it.

Student-teacher

Sometimes a student will want to share or clarify something with the teacher privately. This can be done during a partner-sharing time as described above. This is a good time for you to help students select journal material to be used as a springboard for more public writing, such as essays, poetry, or short stories for school assignments.

Group

Sharing in a group can be done after or instead of partner sharing. Group sharing is the type I most frequently use in my workshops as I find students appreciate hearing other people's comments and journal experiences. You be the judge as to which form of sharing is most appropriate for a particular day or for the exercise you have given.

Group sharing can be done with the entire class or can be done in smaller groups, five to ten in a group. You can circulate from group to group, with perhaps a leader guiding the discussion in each group. *It is very important that there be no judgment or criticism from you or the students toward each other.* In all of the sharing, a safe atmosphere must be maintained, otherwise people edit their journal work or are unwilling to express themselves in a group. It must be emphasized that criticism or judgment, when brought in too early, shuts down the creative process. *Constructive* criticism has its place in the development of writing and art for public display or for class assignments in English, history, or other subjects, but the journal is not for public consumption or evaluation. It is for personal, creative expression, for brainstorming, for loosening up and limbering up the ability to communicate in words and pictures.

ACCOUNTABILITY

I do not believe that actual journal entries should be judged or graded. However, students can be held accountable for keeping a journal or using the journal period productively. They should not be allowed to interfere with others during this period. Students can be asked to write papers in which they describe their journal-keeping progress. What are they learning about themselves? About writing? About drawing? About anything? This kind of *self-evaluation* is the most valuable form of accountability. It gives the student responsibility for his or her own learning and growth. That is one of the most important goals of the Creative Journal Method—personal responsibility.

STORAGE

It is advisable for students to keep the journal in school in as private a place as possible. This safeguards confidentiality and prevents loss, damage, or forgetfulness about bringing the journal to school. Some teachers keep all the journals locked in a cupboard or suggest they be kept in lockers.

REVIEWING THE JOURNAL

A journal is like a yardstick put on the wall for measuring a child's physical growth. The journal is a permanent record of *inner* growth. It can be a highly valuable means for helping a child to see the inevitable development of self-understanding as well as creative abilities and communication skills.

After the children have done journal work for a period of time, ask them to write about the things they are learning about themselves, patterns they see, things they'd like to change. Encourage them to evaluate what the journal means to them and how it functions in their lives.

> This morning when I had nothing to do I turned over some of the pages of my diary. . . . I remained sitting with the open pages in my hand, and thought about it and how it came about. . . . I have been trying to understand the Anne of a year ago. . . . I hid myself within myself, I only considered myself and quietly wrote down all my joys, sorrows, and contempt in my diary. This diary is of great value to me because it has become a book of memoirs in many places, but on a good many pages I could certainly put "past and done with."
>
> I have an odd way of sometimes being able to see myself through someone else's eyes. Then I view the affairs of a certain "Anne" at my ease, and browse through the pages of her life as if she were a stranger.
>
> Anne Frank
> *Diary of a Young Girl*

EDUCATING PARENTS: AN ESSENTIAL PART OF A SCHOOL JOURNAL PROGRAM

It is extremely important for educators to tell parents about their journal program in the schools. In order to prevent misunderstandings about goals and the nature and scope of journal-keeping in the classroom, I suggest that a letter be sent home to all parents of students who are keeping journals in class. The following is a letter an elementary school principal wrote to inform parents about the creative journal program at her school. Write your own version of this, if you like.

This principal emphasized the need to respect the child's privacy and the academic value of journal-keeping, but you may want to address other issues in your letter.

Dear Parents:

Our students are now keeping journals to develop basic skills in language and problem-solving. Students are given journal writing assignments on many topics, including concepts being studied in subject matter areas. On the theory that *practice makes perfect,* our aim is to foster practice and enjoyment in writing by removing fear of criticism. For this reason, the journal is like a diary: it is private and confidential. It is the student's personal possession.

Our rule is: No one may look in another person's journal, not even the teacher or counselor. If a student wants to share something from the journal, that is permitted, but it is strictly voluntary. We ask you to cooperate with this program by respecting our rule and your child's right to privacy in the journal. Although the journals will be kept at school, they will eventually be taken home. Also, some students may want to keep a second journal on their own at home.

Keep in mind that journal-keeping *is not a substitute* for formal writing assignments which are corrected and graded. Rather, the journal is used *in addition* to formal writing. It is a place to practice, to warm up, to write with comfort and ease before having to perform for grades on tests and assignments.

A recent research project using the journal method in the Garvey School District (a multi-cultural district in the San Gabriel Valley), showed great gains in reading and math test scores (as much as 20% points). We are confident that journal-keeping will benefit our students by motivating them to write, by developing basic skills and the self-esteem and confidence that comes with success.

Thank you for helping make this program a success.

Sincerely,
Z.S., *Principal*

Before the program starts, a parent meeting can be very beneficial. Parent support for journal-keeping has contributed greatly to the success of programs established in many public schools. At one elementary school, such involvement resulted in a donation of beautiful hardbound blank books by the employer of one of the parents.

SUGGESTED READINGS

FOR CHILDREN

Center for Attitudinal Healing Staff. *There Is a Rainbow Behind Every Dark Cloud*. Millbrae: Celestial Arts, 1979.

Frank, Anne. *The Diary of a Young Girl*. New York: Doubleday, 1967.

Sendak, Maurice. *Where the Wild Things Are*. New York: Harper & Row, 1964.

———. *Dear Mili*. New York: Farrar, Straus & Giroux, 1988.

Striker, Susan. *The Anti-Coloring Book of Exploring Space on Earth*. New York: Holt, Rinehart & Winston, 1980.

Striker, Susan, and Edward Kimmel. *The Anti-Coloring Book*. New York: Holt, Rinehart & Winston, 1978.

———. *The Second Anti-Coloring Book*. New York: Holt, Rinehart & Winston, 1979.

———. *The Third Anti-Coloring Book*. New York: Holt, Rinehart & Winston, 1980.

———. *The Fourth Anti-Coloring Book*. New York: Holt, Rinehart & Winston, 1981.

———. *The Fifth Anti-Coloring Book*. New York: Holt, Rinehart & Winston, 1982.

———. *The Sixth Anti-Coloring Book*. New York: Holt, Rinehart & Winston, 1984.

FOR PARENTS AND TEACHERS

Brookes, Mona. *Drawing with Children*. Los Angeles: J. P. Tarcher, 1986.

Capacchione, Lucia. *The Creative Journal: The Art of Finding Yourself*. Athens, Ohio; Ohio University/Swallow Press, 1979, 1988.

———. *The Power of Your Other Hand*. North Hollywood, Calif.: Newcastle, 1988.

———. *The Well-Being Journal*. North Hollywood, Calif.: Newcastle, 1989.

Koch, Kenneth. *Wishes, Lies, and Dreams: Teaching Children to Write Poetry*. New York: Harper & Row, 1980.

———. *Rose, Where Did You Get That Red?* New York: Random House, 1974.

Murdock, Maureen. *Spinning Inward*. Boston: Shambhala Publications, 1987.

About Me

The journal starts with the self. The child explores the inner world of feelings, attitudes, and body sensations as well as the outer image of names and activities. From these inward journeys the child comes out of himself or herself through creative expression. By encouraging introspection and self-awareness, we help the child develop greater self-esteem.

> I hope I shall be able to confide in you completely, as I have never been able to do in anyone before, and I hope that you will be a great support and comfort to me.
>
> I have two things to confess to you today, which will take a long time. But I must tell someone and you are the best one to tell, as I know that, come what may, you always keep a secret.
>
> I want to go on living even after my death! And therefore I am grateful to God for giving me this gift, this possibility of developing myself and of writing, of expressing all that is in me.
>
> Anne Frank
> *Diary of a Young Girl*

≪ ≪ ≪ ≪ ≫ ≫ ≫ ≫

Warm-Ups or Scribble-Scrabble

How: Suggest that the child choose a color and make marks on the journal page. Encourage him to scribble, doodle, play around.

If you are working with school-age children, ask them *not* to make "pictures" or planned designs. Tell them the point of this exercise is to "play around" and "warm up." It's like a limbering exercise or like tuning an instrument.

Why: At the earliest age, children begin their paper and pencil expressions by scribbling. Like crawling and making "goo-goo" sounds, which later lead to walking and talking, scribbling is the playful preparation for drawing and writing. Unfortunately, children don't normally get encouragement or practice in scribbling, which adults consider messy, ugly, and meaningless. Scribbling is a wonderful form of emotional release and relaxation. And it's fun! Try it yourself and see what I mean. By actually encouraging doodling and "ugly, messy" scribbling, we help them experience a necessary stage in their creative growth and development, as necessary as crawling and making "goo-goo" sounds.

WHEN: This exercise is a standard one for preschool children at the presymbolic stage of art. They can do it in conjunction with the later exercise "Feelings." It is also helpful for children and adolescents who think they have no talent and feel inadequate in art. These children don't enjoy the *process* of drawing; they have learned only to judge themselves and their art as not measuring up to the standards set in the past by adults. This exercise opens the child up to relaxing; playing around; having fun with colors, lines, and shapes; and expressing spontaneously.

This scribble was drawn by a child holding felt pens of different colors in one hand.

≪ ≪ ≪ ≪ ≫ ≫ ≫ ≫
Doodle Drawings

How: Suggest that the child first make doodles, abstract lines, and shapes on the page without trying to make a "picture" or draw recognizable objects.

Then ask the child if she can find recognizable objects in any of the lines or shapes. Suggest that she outline, color in, or in some way emphasize the parts of the doodle that suggest the object so that it becomes more clear.

If the child has writing skills, ask her to write a poem about all the things she found in her doodle drawing.

Why: Like "Warm-Ups," this exercise encourages a relaxed, playful, adventurous attitude about art and writing. It also develops the ability to visualize, which is so important in written language and aesthetic development.

Even Leonardo da Vinci spoke about the value of finding images in abstract patterns as a stimulus for the imagination. Here is what he said:

> I cannot forbear to mention . . . a new device for study which, although it may seem trivial and almost ludicrous, is nevertheless extremely useful in arousing the mind to various inventions. And this is, when you look at a wall spotted with stains . . . you may discover a resemblance to various landscapes, beautified with mountains, rivers, rocks, trees . . . or again you may see battles and figures in action, or strange faces and costumes and an endless variety of objects which you could reduce to complete and well-drawn forms. And these appear on such walls confusedly, like the sound of bells in whose jangle you may find any name or word you choose to imagine.

When: This is an excellent activity for very young children who have not yet learned to write. When children need to loosen up, this exercise works wonders. Children who have reached the symbolic stage will benefit greatly from this stimulation of visual imagination. The poem is a good springboard for creative thinking in verbal children, since the objects in the picture might be very diverse, and tying them together would require a leap of imagination and a whimsical approach to words and images.

≪ ≪ ≪ ≪ ≫ ≫ ≫ ≫

Free-Drawing

How: Invite the child to draw freely without planning, without copying anything or trying to make "art." Encourage the child to have fun exploring color, line, shape, texture.

If the child can write, ask him to pretend his picture can talk. Suggest that the child give a name to each part of the drawing and let each one speak. What does each shape or color or form say? Have the child write it down.

WHY: This activity helps children interpret their own visual language and expression. It's like having a "dream on paper" and understanding its symbolic meaning. It helps uncover feelings and attitudes in the unconscious. It also helps children drop their performance fears about making "pretty pictures" and encourages them to enjoy the *process* of art.

WHEN: This is another standard journal excercise that can be done every day or as often as possible. It's an excellent warm-up and is a must for children who have been led to believe they can't draw or don't have talent.

≪ ≪ ≪ ≪ ≫ ≫ ≫ ≫

Feelings

How: Ask the child to draw how he feels right now. The drawing might be scribbling, doodling, shapes, lines, textures, images. Suggest that the child choose colors that express his feelings.

After the drawing is done, if the child *can't write,* ask if he can give a word or words that express the feelings in the drawing. If the child is *learning to write,* ask him to dictate a word or description to you. Write it down on a separate card and encourage the child to copy the words into the journal, either on the page with the drawing or on the next page, whichever is appropriate. If the child *can write,* ask him to write down the feelings that he drew.

WHY: Often it is difficult for children to express how they feel in ways acceptable to adults. Certain feelings—anger, sadness, fear, jealousy—are considered "bad" by adults so children hold these feelings in due to fear of rejection or punishment by adults. Because the feeling is labeled "bad," the child thinks he is bad for having the feeling. This has a profoundly negative effect on self-esteem, spontaneity, and creative expression. This exercise allows expression of any and all feelings in a safe place, the journal. We hope the child will learn to accept his feelings *and* himself.

WHEN: This is an excellent exercise to suggest for a child who is having difficulty handling powerful emotions. It is especially useful in the classroom when there isn't the time or the personnel to deal with a child's feelings, but the feelings are coming out in antisocial or violent behavior. It is a perfect tool for getting to *real* feelings and discharging them.

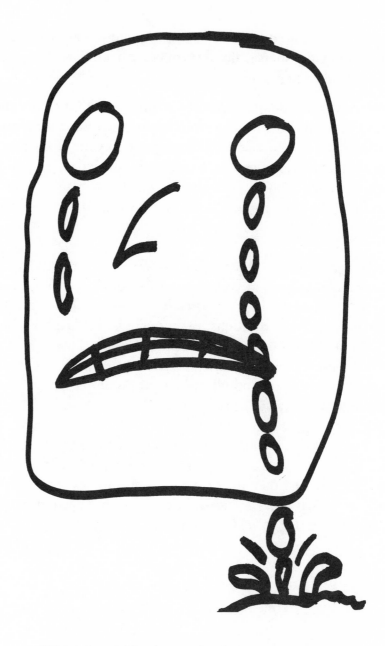

"This is how I felt when my brother ran away. I was mad."

≪ ≪ ≪ ≪ ≫ ≫ ≫ ≫

Who Am I?

How: Suggest that the child draw a self-portrait. It might be a picture of the child's physical appearance or symbols, colors, shapes, or abstract designs.

After the drawing is done, invite the child to write a poem entitled "I Am . . ." It need not rhyme. If a child needs help, suggest beginning each line with "I am _____" and then completing the sentence.

Why: Exploring oneself in words and pictures is a wonderful way to gain self-understanding and confidence. There is nothing more interesting to us than ourselves, so it is a topic with endless possibilities for creative expression. Also, we are all experts on ourselves—no one knows us better than we do—so the drawing and writing done here have the vitality that comes from personal experience.

When: All children can benefit from this exercise, especially those with poor self-concept. The latter group should immediately be given the "Dear Self" exercise, which follows.

"I am David. David feels like he's going to fly up in the air. David's going to fly to run away. It's fun up here! That's all about David the Bird."

≪ ≪ ≪ ≪ ≫ ≫ ≫ ≫

Dear Self

How: Invite the child to write a letter to herself starting with the words "Dear Self." Have the child write all the things she likes about herself as if she were writing to another person.

Why: This is an important technique for raising self-esteem by developing an attitude of pride in one's positive qualities and achievements.

When: When a child's self-confidence is low, for whatever reason, this can be an excellent "pick-me-up." It also encourages the child to value her own opinion of herself, instead of always depending upon what others think about her.

≪ ≪ ≪ ≪ ≫ ≫ ≫ ≫

My Name

How: Suggest that the child create a design using his name and expressing who he is.

If appropriate to the child's level, explain how logos, trademarks, and symbols are used to identify or communicate a group or company. Show examples. Ask the child to create his own *original* logo or symbol.

Variations: Suggest that the child study different typefaces and letter forms in books and magazines for inspiration. Also, different emotions can be expressed through different letter styles and colors. A child could be asked to express how he feels through a name design.

WHY: In this exercise the child can see how his name expresses his personality and one aspect of his identity. It also allows for an appreciation of the aesthetic, expressive quality of letter forms and symbols.

WHEN: This exercise can be done periodically, especially if the variations are used in subsequent uses.

≪ ≪ ≪ ≪ ≫ ≫ ≫ ≫

My Body, Myself

How: Ask the child to draw the outline of her body. Then suggest that she color in any area of her body that hurts or that she thinks of as a problem.

After the drawing is done, ask the child to pretend that the body part that was colored in can speak. What does it say?

1. What is it?
2. How does it feel?
3. Why does it feel that way?
4. What can she do to help it?

If the child can write, ask her to write down what the body part said. Ask her to write it in the first person. The child might even draw a "balloon" (like those in comic strips) coming out of the body part with the words written into it.

Why: This exercise develops body awareness and the ability to listen to one's physical needs. It helps children become more responsible for themselves and understand how emotions are expressed through the body.

When: This exercise can be done anytime. It is especially helpful if a child is feeling ill or has a chronic ailment or physical condition.

≪ ≪ ≪ ≪ ≫ ≫ ≫ ≫

Inside Me, Outside Me

How: Invite the child to draw

    1. how others see him on the outside and
    2. how he feels inside.

If the child can write, suggest that he write about what he sees in his picture. Are there differences between the outside and the inside? What are they and how does he feel about them?

Why: This exercise encourages children to see and express their own feelings even if they are different from what they think others are feeling and expressing.

When: This is an especially good technique to use with children who have difficulty knowing and expressing how they really feel and who often try to please others to win approval.

≪ ≪ ≪ ≪ ≫ ≫ ≫ ≫
My Day

How: Ask the child to draw a picture of the most important thing that happened that day.

If the child can write, have her write down what happened, as shown in the pictures, as well as her feelings about what happened.

Alternates: For "My Week," instead of expressing an event from the day, select one from the past week. "My Weekend" could be done at school at the beginning of the week.

WHY: This exercise develops visual memory and observation skills. It also helps children learn to describe events in the order in which they occur. It encourages children to communicate their experiences and their reactions to events, and it can help them express and resolve feelings about troublesome events.

WHEN: This is a standard journal exercise, and it forms the basis of most diaries. It can be done every day. It can also be done on a weekly basis, although in that case it would need to be done with children advanced enough to understand the duration of a week.

≪ ≪ ≪ ≪ ≫ ≫ ≫ ≫

My Life: History Timeline

How: Suggest that the child draw a timeline (as shown), with her birthdate at the left side and the present year at the right end.

birth_____present

Vertically along the line, the child writes a word or phrase describing important events or experiences in her life with the year and/or the child's age written on the timeline.

After doing the timeline, the child is ready to do the next exercise: "My Story." If the child cannot write, suggest that she draw a picture history of the important events or experiences.

Why: This is an excellent preparation for the autobiographical writing in the next exercises. It also helps children learn a sense of history and sequence of time based on their own experiences.

When: This exercise is appropriate for children who have, or are developing, an understanding of time and the ordering of events in sequence. It is especially useful for children who are studying history.

≪ ≪ ≪ ≪ ≫ ≫ ≫ ≫

My Story: Autobiography

How: Ask the child to write his life story, starting at the beginning and going up to the present.

Suggest that the child read over what he has written and select one thing to illustrate by drawing a picture of it.

The child might then write more details about the "scene" shown in the illustration.

Later, more drawings can be done to illustrate other parts of the written autobiography.

Why: Here is a perfect opportunity for a child to learn communication skills by expressing what he knows best: personal experience. It gives the child a chance to engage in self-reflection, to gain insight into the meaning of events in everyday life, and to develop skills in recall, descriptive writing, and drawing. It also gives the child a sense of sequential order and "history."

When: This is an exercise that can be done in installments. The autobiography can be deepened and expanded indefinitely through drawing and more detailed writing about each episode or scene.

My Story

I have never really sat down and thought about my past. I've had happiness and sadness like other people. I've lived in 5 states and moved 15 times. I've traveled and done a lot of things. My parents were divorced when I was six, and my Mother and I moved to my Grandma's. I was then an only child. I got to visit my Father once a year, but it wasn't the same. I kinda grew up without a father. He always wanted me to be musical and artistic, so I took piano, dance and voice lessons, etc. With them, I got to perform a lot. I've always been involved in something, very busy. I've even won contests, mostly drawing. When I was 11 my mother remarried, and we moved to a new house. Now, I have a little brother, and I'm not an only child anymore.

THREE

How I Feel, What I Think

≪ ≪ ≪ ≪ ≪ ≫ ≫ ≫ ≫ ≫

Children (and adults) feel emotions all the time. A very important part of knowing ourselves and each other is knowing how we feel and what we think and sharing ourselves with others.

Feelings are personal, and yet they are common to all humans. Learning to communicate how we feel to ourselves, first, can help us communicate better with others.

> I am boiling with rage . . . I'd like to stamp my feet, scream, give Mummy a good shaking, cry, and I don't know what else. . . .
>
> I really ought not to write this . . . but still, whatever you think of me, I can't keep everything to myself, so I'll remind you of my opening words—"Paper is patient!"
>
> But, still, the brightest spot of all is that at least I can write down my thoughts and feelings, otherwise I would be absolutely stifled!
>
> I can shake off everything if I write; my sorrows disappear, my courage is reborn. . . .
>
> Anne Frank
> *Diary of a Young Girl*

≪ ≪ ≪ ≪ ≫ ≫ ≫ ≫

Happiness Is . . .

How:

Drawing: Suggest that the child draw a picture of what it's like to be happy, using colors and scribbles, shapes, lines, or images that express happiness.

Writing: If the child can write, invite him to write about all the things he feels happy about. If the child is learning to write, he can dictate words that go with the drawing. Write them down on separate cards for him to learn and copy into the journal if he wishes.

Lists: Young children can make lists headed with the following categories: *People, Places, Things, Activities (I Feel Happy About)*. Older children can be guided into describing in depth something that made them feel happy today.

Poetry: Poems can be written by repeating and completing the line "Happiness is . . ."

Illustrations: Invite the child to illustrate the things or images contained in any of the writings.

WHY: This activity helps children learn to express their feelings both verbally and nonverbally. It encourages exploration of emotions and how they are related to everyday life.

WHEN: The prose part of this exercise can be done every day, along with an illustration of what was described. The other parts can be selected and done periodically, depending on the level and interest of the child. Happy feelings will undoubtedly be expressed from time to time in the Chapter 2 exercise "Feelings." If you know a child is happy at the time, "Happiness Is . . ." would be a good follow-up exercise, since it allows for a more in-depth exploration than the "Feelings" exercise does.

≪ ≪ ≪ ≫ ≫ ≫ ≫

I'm Scared

How: Ask the child to draw a picture of something she's afraid of. It can be what scares her the most or what scares her right now, if there's a current situation that is frightening.

If the child can write, invite her to write about all the things that scare her.

A poem about fear can be created. There is no need to rhyme. If the child has any difficulty, suggest repetition of a phrase to begin each line or group of lines, such as, "It scares me when_____" or "I'm afraid of_____."

Suggest that the child write about what she does when she's afraid. This can also be done as a poem called "When I'm scared . . ."

Invite the child to draw a picture of herself being afraid. The drawing should include the person, thing, or situation she's afraid of. Then ask the child to draw a second picture in which there is a happy ending, for example, she's conquered her fear in some way, made friends with the thing she feared, or solved a problem.

If the child can write, ask her to have a talk with something she's afraid of and write it out like a little play. It could even be done as a cartoon strip with word bubbles showing the dialogue.

Why: Children are often told to be brave and stop being afraid, as if fear were bad. This exercise helps children accept this difficult yet frequently felt emotion by freely expressing it. This way they face the things they fear instead of denying or avoiding them. It also provides an opportunity to imagine new ways to deal with fearful things.

When: When a child is experiencing fearful feelings, fantasies, or recurring dreams, this activity can be most helpful. It is also good as a standard exercise to be done regularly, that is, weekly or monthly, since fear is an emotion that comes up all the time.

≪ ≪ ≪ ≪ ≫ ≫ ≫ ≫

Good and Mad

How: Tell the child that anger can be expressed in many different ways: in pictures, in spoken words, in written words. Ask the child to choose a color or colors that express anger. He can draw what it's like to be mad by scribbling those feelings out on paper in the journal. Encourage freedom of expression and acceptance of angry feelings. The child may want to do many "angry" scribbles.

If the child can write, after the scribbling suggest that he write the angry feelings out in words. Any words are okay. It is very important that the child know that, and also that he know that no one will read what he writes unless he wants them to.

Suggest that the child write in the journal a letter to someone he's angry at, telling the person exactly how he feels.

Why: Anger is one of the most difficult emotions, since it is often associated with loss of approval or violence. The fear of destructive, violent behavior has led to denial or suppression of angry feelings themselves. The very denial or suppression of angry feelings creates a pressure-cooker emotional state, which is likely to explode into the angry, uncontrollable outbursts we fear so much.

We can help children feel okay about their angry feelings by allowing them to verbalize those feelings in the journal. We hope children will be able to express anger verbally instead of stuffing their feelings in or exploding in physical violence or other antisocial behavior. Instead of defacing walls with graffiti (which is really a public form of emotional release) children and young people can learn to use journals.

When: This is an excellent activity for a child who is having trouble with anger, because he's either holding it in or exploding uncontrollably in violent or antisocial behavior.

"I'm mad today. I ran away."

≪ ≪ ≪ ≪ ≫ ≫ ≫ ≫

Color Me Sad

How: Invite the child to draw a picture of sadness. It can be abstract shapes and colors or a picture of herself at a time when she was sad.

If she can write, ask the child to write about the "sad" picture. What does she see there? If a situation was drawn, what happened?

Suggest that the child write a poem, "When I'm Sad . . . ," which tells what she does or doesn't do when she's sad, what happens, and so forth.

Then invite the child to write about a time when a person or people around her were sad. What made them sad? How did she know they were sad? What did they do to show it? What did she do?

Why: Sadness is a difficult emotion; many children are taught to hide it or deny it. "Don't cry" is a command children hear all the time. In this exercise, the child has a chance to explore sadness, its causes, and its expression. We hope she can come to accept sadness as a necessary emotion. The ability to experience her own sadness can also help develop compassion for and acceptance of the sadness of others.

When: If a child is showing deep sadness in body language or conversation, this exercise can be very helpful. It can assist the child in going into the sadness, feeling it, and then moving out of it naturally.

≪ ≪ ≪ ≪ ≫ ≫ ≫ ≫

All Alone

How: Discuss loneliness with the child, sharing your own experiences. Suggest that the child draw a picture of loneliness and what it feels like to be lonely.

If the child can write, suggest that he write about what he sees in his picture.

Invite him to write about times when he felt lonely (it might even be happening now) and why he felt lonely.

Suggest that the child write down what kinds of emotions he feels when he's lonely, and what he does when he's lonely. He might consider writing this as a poem.

Why: Everyone feels lonely at times. Often we try to run away from loneliness instead of using it as a time for self-reflection and an appreciation of solitude. In fact, it is out of fear of loneliness (interpreted as rejection) that we put up with negative situations and behavior from others. The journal is perhaps one of the very best means for dealing with loneliness by learning how to know ourselves better.

When: This activity is perfect for a child who appears to be very dependent upon others and will do anything to avoid being alone. It can also be valuable in the event of a death, a separation or divorce in the family, or a friend moving away.

≪ ≪ ≪ ≪ ≫ ≫ ≫ ≫

Drawing Myself Out

How: Suggest that the child draw images of anything that comes to mind. The point is not to make "art" or a "pretty picture" but simply to let anything come out on the paper, to let one's hand do the "thinking." Tell the child this is like having a dream on paper; it doesn't have to make sense or be realistic.

If the child can write, after she has done some drawing invite her to write about what she sees in her drawings.

Why: This activity helps children loosen up and develop intuition and creativity. It frees the unconscious mind to express itself and promotes a relaxed attitude about nonrational forms of expression.

When: This exercise can be done regularly, even on a daily basis. Like the first four exercises in Chapter 1, it is a great warm-up activity.

≪ ≪ ≪ ≪ ≫ ≫ ≫ ≫
Off the Top of My Head

How: Suggest that the child write anything that comes to mind without trying to make sense, create sentences, or follow rules of grammar. Explain that this is called "free-writing" and that anything goes.

Afterward, suggest that if any interesting images came out in the writing, the child may want to draw pictures of them.

WHY: Like "Drawing Myself Out," this exercise is a great warm-up. It encourages intuitive, stream-of-consciousness expression in words and develops an appreciation for varieties of styles in writing. For older youngsters, the reading of some stream-of-consciousness writing from an author might be appropriate.

WHEN: This exercise can be done frequently since it is such a good warm-up. It is especially helpful for anyone with writer's block or timidity about writing at all.

≪ ≪ ≪ ≪ ≫ ≫ ≫ ≫

One Thing Leads to Another

How: Ask the child to choose a "theme" that is important to him at this time and to pick a word that best expresses the theme.

Alternate: Ask the child to pick his favorite word or the word for his favorite thing.

Tell the child that he can do *free-association* writing on his word theme. Suggest that the child write down his chosen word and follow that with any word that comes to mind and then another word and so on . . . in a chain reaction. One word suggests the next word and that word in turn brings another word to mind and so on until the child feels finished. Explain that these words are not supposed to form sentences or make sense.

WHY: Like the previous two exercises, this activity is a good warm-up and helps develop intuitive, creative abilities by opening up the unconscious mind. It also promotes self-exploration through reflection on one's values.

WHEN: This exercise is especially helpful for children who have difficulty expressing themselves in words. It can also be used as part of a values clarification study.

≪ ≪ ≪ ≪ ≫ ≫ ≫ ≫

Silly Songs

How: Invite the child to play with words and write nonsense poems in which words rhyme, sound alike, or sound funny. When put together the words don't have to mean anything at all. The words can tell about preposterous things and events. A good example to share is Lewis Carroll's poem "Jabberwocky" in *Through the Looking Glass.* Other good examples are the books by Dr. Seuss, in which rhyming and alliteration are used in combination with silly characteristics and situations.

Alternative: Suggest the child write her own silly words to a melody that she already knows.

Why: This is another good warm-up and loosening-up activity. It helps the child have fun with verbal expression and opens up imagination and a sense of adventure with words.

When: Children of all ages enjoy being silly and playing with words and ideas. This exercise is especially valuable when a group of children are in a playful mood and can create poems orally and share in the spontaneous creation of silly songs.

≪ ≪ ≪ ≪ ≫ ≫ ≫ ≫

I Need

How: Ask the child to write a poem called "I Need," which tells about all the things he needs in his life, including people, places, pets, things, activities, and qualities. He is describing all the things that are most important to him. Point out that the poem need not rhyme but can be written in free verse.

WHY: In this exercise, the child is reflecting upon his own values and developing an appreciation of his own opinions and experiences. This is a very important part of building self-awareness and self-respect.

WHEN: This is a valuable exercise for children with low self-esteem and an inability to know what they need or how to ask for it. It can be especially useful for a child who has trouble communicating verbally and therefore resorts to physical or emotional "acting out."

I Need

I need . . .
Love above all
 to love myself and be
  a good friend to myself.

I need . . .
to be touched by something
 outside myself
  both physically and spiritually.

I need . . .
to move my body . . .
 to dance
  or do Tai Chi
   or move my body in some way.

I need . . .
to let my creativity out . . .
 to let myself out . . .
  with what is around me.
   input and output.

I need air
 and nature
  and to understand and experience
   the origins of the world . . .
    the forests, the life . . .

I need freedom
 to live my life
  as I see fit
   to go outside for walks
    at night if I want . . .
     to run my own existence.

I need . . .
 to be me and be allowed to be me.

First published in Lucia Capacchione, *The Creative Journal: The Art of Finding Your-self* (Athens, Ohio: Ohio University/Swallow Press, 1979, 1988). Reprinted with the permission of The Ohio University Press, Athens.

≪ ≪ ≪ ≪ ≫ ≫ ≫ ≫

I Want

How: Suggest to the child that she draw a picture of all the things she wants to have or do in her life.

If the child can write, invite her to make a list called "I Want . . ." It can include things, experiences, activities, qualities, achievements, and so forth.

After the list is written, suggest that the child select one item she can "make happen" now. Ask her to write down all the things she can do to make it happen.

After she has written about it, ask the child to imagine herself having gotten what she wanted. Suggest that she draw a picture of herself enjoying it.

Why: Often children feel like powerless victims whose lives are controlled by grown-ups. This exercise helps children realize the power they have to get what they want. It trains them in positive visualization. It also helps them clarify what is important to them and know that there are steps that can be taken to achieve their goals. This is creative problem solving. This exercise helps train children to know what they want and to ask for it in words instead of resorting to manipulation or violence or withdrawing in frustration.

When: Like the preceding exercise, this is very good for children with poor self-concept. It is also beneficial for children who feel helpless and hopeless.

≪ ≪ ≪ ≪ ≫ ≫ ≫ ≫

My Best Friend

How: Ask the child to think of her best friend. Encourage her to *see* her friend in her mind. What does her friend look like? Do this for a few minutes. Then suggest she draw a picture of the friend

After the picture is drawn, invite the child to write about her friend, including the friend's name, a description of how he or she looks and acts, and any other characteristics. The child can also be guided to write her feelings about the friendship, why she likes this friend best, what she and her friend share or have in common, what they like to do together, and so forth.

Invite the child to do a drawing of herself and her friend doing something together.

Why: Drawing or writing about what we know best is perhaps the best way to practice both of these communication skills, especially if the subject is someone or something of which we are fond. This exercise helps develop the skill of visualization, so important for descriptive writing. It also fosters attention to detail in written expression.

When: This exercise can be done on a regular basis. If done frequently, variations should be introduced by changing the theme to anyone in the child's everyday life, such as relative or neighbor.

I like Kalilah becaus I knew her †since I was born.

≪ ≪ ≪ ≪ ≫ ≫ ≫ ≫

My Hero, My Heroine

How: Discuss the concept of a hero or heroine as someone we admire, respect, and imitate. Give examples of some of your own heroes and heroines. Suggest that the child draw a picture of his current hero or heroine.

Afterward, suggest that the child write down all the qualities, achievements, and so forth that he admires about the hero or heroine.

Then ask the child to have an imaginary conversation with the hero or heroine and to write down what was said. This can be written down as a play script. If there is something the child needs help with in his life, suggest that he ask his hero or heroine for advice and assistance.

Mickey Mouse

WHY: This exercise develops visualization skills. It also fosters the powers of imagination for creating dialogue. It is an important tool for exploring personal values and goals and for internalizing qualities the child is projecting onto the heroic figure.

WHEN: This exercise can be done periodically. If done frequently, you can vary it, for example, by using historical figures or characters from literature as a springboard. The person written about, however, must genuinely be held as heroic by the child; it must not be imposed by the adult.

≪ ≪ ≪ ≪ ≫ ≫ ≫ ≫

A Very Important Person

How: Suggest that the child think of the most important person in her life right now. It could be someone she loves or someone with whom she is having a problem. It could also be someone who is gone or dead. Ask the child to close her eyes for a few moments and picture the person in her mind, what the person looks like, how the person dresses, and so forth.

Invite the child to draw a picture of the important person.

Afterward, suggest that the child write down what this important person would say about himself or herself. It should be written in the *first person,* that is, "My name is ＿＿＿＿＿ and I ＿＿＿＿＿." Let the person describe how he or she feels and thinks.

Then invite the child to tell the important person anything she'd like to say and to write it out.

Why: In this activity, the child gets to experience what it's like to be in another person's shoes. She expands her ability to visualize and characterize a person in drawn and written form. She learns compassion and human understanding.

When: This exercise can be done frequently and is especially valuable in dealing with problems in interpersonal relations. The important person will usually be different each time the exercise is done if you emphasize the "right now" aspect, as directed in the instructions.

2.) My FAVORITE Person

My DAD

Why He's my Favorite Person...

He knows what I'm saying,
when I'm not even talking.
He understands when no one else
does.
He takes the time to listen, whatever big or
small the reason.

He takes the time to be with me, when
there is no time.
We share dreams, hopes, and joys
My DAD and I are like one.

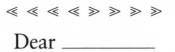

Dear _____

How: Invite the child to write a letter to someone but to write it in the journal. It can be a letter to anyone—a friend or relative, adult or child, even someone the child doesn't know personally. In the letter, the child can say anything he wants to the other person. The letter will not be sent, so the child has the freedom to be completely honest and spontaneous.

Why: Letter writing is an important form of communication and a wonderful way to practice writing. People frequently stop themselves from writing letters because of self-criticism about their writing style. This is an excellent way to practice writing letters without the burden of self-judgment and performance fears.

When: This exercise can be done as frequently as the child wishes. In school it can be done as part of building skill in letter writing, but journal letters should never be graded. They are to be used as practice only. At home, journal letters can be good preparation for writing formal letters to relatives and friends who are away. Like the last exercise, this one can be very helpful in dealing with interpersonal problems. Sometimes the journal-keeper even chooses to copy the letter out, polish it up, and send it.

≪ ≪ ≪ ≪ ≫ ≫ ≫ ≫

Imaginary Friend

How: Suggest that the child create a make-believe friend and draw a picture of him or her. The friend might even be an animal.

After drawing the picture, the child can let the imaginary friend talk in writing, using the first person. The friend introduces him- or herself by name and then answers questions the child asks. This can all be written out like a script for a play, as follows:

Child: _____

Imaginary Friend: _____

Child: _____

Imaginary Friend: _____
(etc.)

Why: Many children have imaginary friends, but because "make-believe" isn't valued by adults, children are discouraged from talking about this form of fantasy. In this exercise, the child not only accepts his imagination but also uses it as a springboard for art and verbal communication. This exercise also helps the child integrate into his own personality the qualities being projected onto the imaginary character.

When: This activity can be useful if a child already has an imaginary friend. It can also help children who need and want to expand their imaginations.

≪ ≪ ≪ ≪ ≫ ≫ ≫ ≫
Count Your Blessings

How: Ask the child to think about all the people who help her, adults and children alike. Then suggest that she make a diagram showing herself and all these people. It might be a simple cartoon showing how they help her.

Invite the child to write the names of the helpers and how each person helps her. Then suggest that she write a sentence or more to each helper, expressing thanks.

Afterward, suggest that the child write a list of all the things she is grateful for.

WHY: Developing a sense of appreciation and gratitude is an important part of social growth. This exercise encourages not only an appreciation of others but also the ability to communicate such feelings.

WHEN: In the classroom, this exercise can be introduced with group discussion and followed up with a thank-you letter assignment, especially if children are learning about letter writing. This exercise is especially appropriate at Thanksgiving or other holiday seasons.

≪ ≪ ≪ ≪ ≫ ≫ ≫ ≫

A Helping Hand

How: Ask the child to think about all the people, animals, or plants that he helps or takes care of. Suggest that he draw pictures of some of them.

Then ask him to write a list of as many things as he can think of that fall into this category. Suggest that after each item he write a sentence or more telling how he helps that particular person, animal, or plant.

Why: This exercise helps develop the child's awareness of the needs of others and a sense of himself as a socially responsible being.

When: This exercise can be done on a fairly regular basis. It is especially useful with children who have difficulty socializing with others. It can help them out of their self-conscious withdrawal and into an awareness and appreciation of others.

≪ ≪ ≪ ≪ ≫ ≫ ≫ ≫

A Family Portrait

How: Suggest that the child draw a picture of herself with her family. This can be an extended family, two families (in the case of divorce), or just the family members with whom she lives. Include animals and pets, if there are any.

Afterward, ask the child to have each family member pictured tell his or her name and something about himself or herself. This can be done in balloons (like the ones seen in cartoons) or it can be written under the pictures.

Why: This exercise fosters a sense of individual differences and family bonds, an appreciation for individuality and commonality found in the child's family of origin as well as the "family of man." It also encourages a better understanding of the people in the child's family.

When: Whenever there is a change in family composition, such as the birth of a baby, divorce, or death, it is especially beneficial for the child to do this exercise.

≪ ≪ ≪ ≪ ≫ ≫ ≫ ≫

Family Tree

How: Using the example shown below, ask the child to make a family tree diagram. Ask her to fill in the names of each family member.

Invite the child to draw a family tree picture in any way she chooses, showing family members through drawings, cartoons, or symbols.

Then suggest that the child write something about each person included in the diagram.

Why: This activity develops a sense of one's roots and origins. It encourages an appreciation of family bonds and relationships.

When: Once this exercise has been done, it is not necessary to do it again unless there is a change in family composition such as birth, death, or divorce.

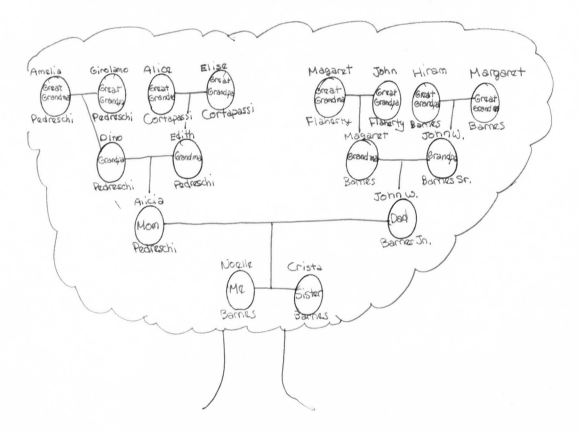

≪ ≪ ≪ ≪ ≫ ≫ ≫ ≫

The Family That Plays Together

How: Ask the child to draw a picture of himself and his family doing something enjoyable together. If there are two families, due to a divorce, the child might want to draw two pictures. He can write about what he drew in the picture(s).

Suggest that the child make a list of things he likes to do with his family (activities at home, outings, vacations, and so on).

Why: This exercise encourages a sense of personal desires and values and the ability to communicate them to others. It also develops self-worth, an appreciation of what makes the child happy, and how he can achieve enjoyment with others.

When: This is a very good exercise to do before or after weekends or vacation periods, when children usually have more time with their families.

My Birthday Party

We had my birthday party outside. We played basketball. There were a lot of people. They gave me $4.00 and 2 Tonka Toys and 1 other game. We had cake and a big sandwich and ice cream and tomato juice. Even my next door neighbor came. We still have some part of the sandwich and cake left.

≪ ≪ ≪ ≪ ≫ ≫ ≫ ≫

Likes and Dislikes

How: Suggest that the child write a poem about things she likes (people, things, activities, foods, and so forth). The poem can be titled "I Like . . ." It need not rhyme.

Suggest that the child illustrate the poem with one item and write about why she likes the thing she drew.

Invite the child to write a second poem about things she doesn't like and title it: "I Don't Like . . ." The categories listed above can be used.

Afterward, the child can illustrate the poem and write about why she doesn't like the things pictured.

Why: Having feelings and opinions and expressing them is a sign of self-esteem. This exercise helps children examine their feelings and experiences and communicate them.

When: Obviously, this exercise is suited for children who can write. It is very helpful for children who are shy and have difficulty expressing their opinions.

I Like	*I Dislike*
Ice cream	Pepperoni
Smurfs	Boxing
Soccer	Basketball
Baseball	Cold Weather
Roller Skating	Peppers
Football	Being Bored
Movies	Bees
Snow	(a house) Fire
Gymnastics	Cuts (on me)
Roses	Mean Dogs
Nice Dogs	(seeing) Blood
Writing things like this!	

≪ ≪ ≪ ≪ ≫ ≫ ≫ ≫

What I Like to Do

How: Suggest that the child draw a picture of himself doing something he likes to do.

If the child can write, ask him to write down why he likes to do what he drew in the picture. How does he feel when he does it?

Why: Being aware of what they like can help children increase their sense of self-worth. Expressing what they like stimulates attention to detail and to feelings and improves the ability to communicate experiences.

When: This is another standard journal exercise that can be done frequently, perhaps weekly. It is appropriate for children who have achieved the "pictorial stage" in art, that is, the ability to show events through pictures or representational symbols.

What I Like to Do

Music fills me with a flood of happiness every time I hear it. The music surrounds me, puts me into my own little world, which no one can penetrate. It relaxes me, making me feel free of responsibilities and cares for just a moment. It gives me a chance to express myself. It's like a miracle medicine, releasing my anger, sorrow, even joy, making me feel better. Music gives me a feeling of weightlessness. I love music!

I Like to Listen to Music

Around Me

≪ ≪ ≪ ≪ ≪ ≫ ≫ ≫ ≫ ≫

I cannot improve on Anne Frank's words on awareness of the world around us and, especially, of nature.

> When I looked outside at night into the depth of Nature and God, then I was happy, really happy . . . so long as I have that happiness here, the joy in nature, health and a lot more besides, all the while one has that, one can always recapture happiness.
>
> Riches can all be lost, but that happiness in your heart can only be veiled, and it can still bring you happiness again, as long as you live. As long as you can look fearlessly up into the heavens, as long as you know that you are pure within and that you will still find happiness.
>
> The best remedy for those who are afraid, lonely, or unhappy is to go outside, somewhere where they can be quiet alone with the heavens, nature, and God. Because only then does one feel that all is as it should be and that God wishes to see people happy, amidst the simple beauty of nature. As long as this exists, and it certainly always will, I know then that there will always be comfort for every sorrow, whatever the circumstance may be. And I firmly believe that nature brings solace in all troubles.
>
> Anne Frank
> *Diary of a Young Girl*

≪ ≪ ≪ ≪ ≫ ≫ ≫ ≫

My Favorite Thing

How: Ask the child to think about his favorite thing. Suggest that he close his eyes and picture it in his mind. What shape is it? What size? What color? What texture?

Suggest that the child draw a picture of his favorite thing. He can draw it from memory or, if it is available, he can draw it from life.

Note: If the child has any insecurity about his ability to draw representationally, point out that his drawing is not for other people but is a way to show appreciation for his favorite thing. By taking the time to think about it and draw it lovingly, the child is communicating with it.

After the drawing is complete, suggest that the child tell the favorite thing how he feels about it and why.

Next, ask the child to pretend that the favorite thing can talk. What would it say? Ask him to write it down.

Why: This exercise develops a sense of appreciation for the things that are useful and pleasurable to us. It is also helpful for children who take material things for granted or whose sense of values about physical reality is distorted into destructiveness or greed, boredom, or selfishness. This is also a wonderful way to motivate drawing. Choosing something one loves and then drawing it encourages expressive art from the heart. When art is done with true feeling, it has a life and vitality that goes beyond technique or learned skill. This is an especially important exercise for children who feel they don't have talent or "can't draw a straight line."

When: This activity can be done on a regular basis, perhaps once a week, as a method for developing visual awareness and abilities in art.

"My stuffed animal Smurfette is definitely my favorite
thing. With her blue skin and yellow hair she's very
lovable."

Something I'd Like to Have

How: Suggest that the child close her eyes and think about something she'd like to have. It may be a pet, a plant, an object, something to wear, or a musical instrument. Ask the child to picture the thing in her mind. What does it look like? What is its size, color, shape, texture, and so forth?

Ask the child to open her eyes and draw a picture of the thing she'd like to have.

Afterward, suggest that the child write about why she wants it and what she would do with it or how she would enjoy it.

Why: This is good training in visualization, which is important for basic learning. This exercise will also help the child become more observant of physical properties and details and be able to express them in art and writing.

When: This exercise can be done as an alternative to "My Favorite Thing" and can be done periodically.

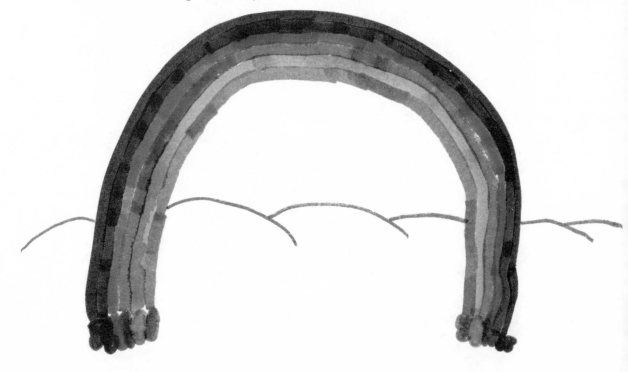

≪ ≪ ≪ ≪ ≫ ≫ ≫ ≫

My House: Inside and Out

How: Ask the child to draw a picture of the house where he lives. Start with a picture of the outside of the house. Then suggest a second picture showing the inside of the house. This second picture might be a drawing of one room and might include family members. The child might also do a floor plan of the entire house, depending on his own developmental level and interest.

Why: In this activity, the child is learning to remember and reproduce visual images from everyday experiences. Often these images are taken for granted or overlooked, but because they are familiar they can provide raw material for all kinds of creative expression.

Since the house is often interpreted psychologically as a symbol for the self, this exercise can help a child develop greater self-awareness and an appreciation of his own needs.

When: This activity is especially useful when a child is about to move or has recently moved to a new residence.

≪ ≪ ≪ ≪ ≫ ≫ ≫ ≫

My Room

How: Suggest that the child draw a picture of herself in her room at home. If she shares her room with others, she might include them in the picture or just draw herself in her area of the room. Leave it up to the child.

After doing the drawing, the child can be guided to write what she likes and doesn't like about her room.

Then suggest a drawing of how she'd like the room (or her area of it) to be.

Why: Like the previous activities, this one heightens the child's ability to observe physical details and to reproduce them visually. It also develops the child's awareness of her needs, her environment, and the part of it that reflects or expresses her own personality, her likes and dislikes.

When: This activity can be done periodically. It can be very useful when a family is planning to move or has recently moved to another home. It is especially important for adolescents, who are developing a sense of their own values and tastes.

≪ ≪ ≪ ≪ ≫ ≫ ≫ ≫

My School

How: Suggest that the child draw a picture of his school. He may include himself in the picture if he wishes. He can draw the picture from memory or draw a particular view of the school by looking at it.

After completing the drawing, ask the child to write about school, how he feels about school, what he likes and doesn't like about it, what he does there. If he could change anything about school, what would it be and how would he change it?

WHY: In this activity, the child is observing all aspects of the environment in which he spends so much time. This exercise helps him reflect on his own personal experience and develops his own sense of values, needs, and wants. This is rare in many school situations, where children are expected to defer to the needs of authority figures and follow the instructions and values of others without question.

WHEN: This activity need not be done frequently, perhaps once a semester. It is an important activity for a child who has recently changed schools.

≪ ≪ ≪ ≪ ≫ ≫ ≫ ≫

My Classroom

How: Suggest that the child draw a picture of herself in her classroom at school. If she has more than one classroom, that is, different classrooms for different subjects, then ask her to select one room and draw it. She may want to do more drawings later if she has more than one classroom.

Afterward, ask the child to write about the other people and activities in the classroom. Suggest that she write about what she likes and what she doesn't like.

WHY: This activity encourages attention to details in the child's daily environment and develops the ability to communicate her attitudes and reactions to the surroundings and other people.

WHEN: This exercise can be done each semester or whenever a child changes classroom environments.

≪ ≪ ≪ ≪ ≫ ≫ ≫ ≫

A Place in Nature

How: Ask the child to close his eyes and imagine he can go to a place in nature. Have him pick a place he's visited and pretend he is there, looking at everything, moving around. Where is he? What does he see? Is it daytime or nighttime? What is the weather like? What is it like to be there and to move around there? Are there other people or animals there?

Suggest that the child open his eyes and draw a picture of the place he saw in his imagination.

Then ask the child to write about the place and to describe it. When he went there, was he alone or with others? What did he do when he went there? How did he feel going there in his imagination?

Why: This exercise reinforces the child's ability to visualize and use his imagination. It encourages him to remember details and to express his observations in drawing and writing. It also helps develop an appreciation of natural beauty.

When: This exercise can be done frequently. It is especially appropriate on or after an outing or vacation to a natural setting, or as a follow-up activity to a class field trip. Journal work can be a valuable activity when children are traveling, as they often get restless in cars, buses, or planes and need something to occupy their attention.

≪ ≪ ≪ ≪ ≫ ≫ ≫ ≫

A Special Place

How: Ask the child to close her eyes and imagine that she is in a very special place she's been where she truly enjoyed herself. Ask her to return there in her imagination, to move around and look around at everything. This may be someone's house, a church, restaurant, amusement park, or some other place.

Suggest that the child open her eyes and draw a picture of herself in the special place.

Then suggest that she write about the place. Where was it? What did she do when she went there in her imagination? How did she feel about the place?

Why: Visualization is an important part of imagination. It also helps develop the sensitivity to images, impressions, and details in the physical environment that form the basis for creative writing and drawing.

When: This activity can be done quite frequently, especially after an outing, vacation, or field trip.

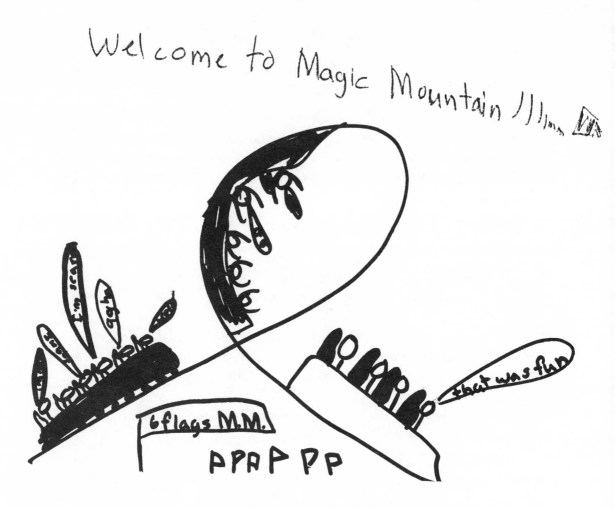

Magic Mountain

The ride is called The Revolution. I was scared! I put my head under the seat when we were on top of the circle. My stomach had butterflies in it. My friend Joanne said it was wonderful.

I thought if I yelled I'd fall out because of the vibration, so I was quiet.

I felt better when we got off.

≪ ≪ ≪ ≪ ≫ ≫ ≫ ≫

My World: A Magic Circle

How: Explain that in this activity the child will make a mandala. The word *mandala* means circle in Sanskrit. It is a circular design that radiates out from a center. In nature, typical mandala designs are the eye or a flower with petals around a center. A common example of a mandala is the rose window in Gothic churches. Discuss other mandala forms that the child may be familiar with such as clocks, compasses, and other circular forms.

Ask the child to draw a large circle on the page as the outline or frame for the mandala. The circle can fill the entire page. Then have the child make a dot in the center of the circle and imagine she is there, where the dot is. Suggest that she draw some symbol for herself in that central spot on the page.

Then ask the child to draw her world in images, shapes, colors, or lines coming outward from the center. This design can be an abstract design or it could include recognizable objects or symbols. The important thing is that the parts are all radiating out from the center in a circular design.

WHY: The mandala is an ancient design motif and appears in the art and architecture of all cultures throughout history. In world religions it has been used as a symbol of unity and focus for meditation. In some forms of psychotherapy it is used for "centering," that is, experiencing the self as the center of one's world. Mandalas have been shown to have a soothing effect on the individual who makes them and who contemplates them. It can help children focus their attention within and feel calm and collected.

WHEN: This exercise can be done regularly. It is excellent for children who are chronically hyperactive or have a short attention span. After free-drawing and emotional release (see Chapter 2), such children can be guided into a mandala activity.

≪ ≪ ≪ ≪ ≫ ≫ ≫ ≫

Vacation

How: Ask the child to write about her vacation, where she went and with whom, what she did, what she liked best, and special things that happened.

Then suggest she draw a picture of the place or event or experience she liked best on the vacation.

Why: This exercise encourages powers of observation, recall, and expression.

When: This is an excellent follow-up activity after a vacation, but it can also be done during the vacation, if it is a lengthy one. Children get restless while traveling, and having a journal along as a companion can be very worthwhile.

Magic Carpet Ride

How: Ask the child to imagine that he has a magic carpet that will take him wherever he wants to go, anywhere in the world or the universe. Ask him to close his eyes and pretend he's on the magic carpet riding through the air. He rides and rides and finally comes to the place of his choice. Ask him to imagine he is landing there. Where is he? What does he see? What does he do? (Allow five to ten minutes for this imagination trip.)

Then ask the child to imagine he is returning from the trip.

Ask him to open his eyes and draw a picture of himself and the place he visited.

Then suggest that he write about what he saw, what he did, and how he felt about the trip.

Why: This exercise further develops imagination and the ability to communicate visual images. It is especially helpful for children who tend to fall back on stereotypical picture symbols or who have difficulty using their imagination.

When: This activity can be used often, perhaps every couple of weeks or so, and can be used in the classroom as part of social studies, geography, or history.

≪ ≪ ≪ ≪ ≫ ≫ ≫ ≫

Land of Make-Believe

How: Ask the child to close her eyes and imagine a land of make-believe. This is a place that the child creates with her imagination. It can be peopled by humans, animals, or imaginary creatures. Anything is possible in this land. Suggest that the child picture it in her mind and move about there. Allow five to ten minutes or more so that she has time to create visual images, conversations, or events.

Note: If the child has difficulty imagining a make-believe land, tell her about, or read aloud from, *Alice in Wonderland, Through the Looking Glass,* or other classics with the theme of make-believe lands.

Ask the child to open her eyes and draw a picture of her make-believe land.

Then ask her to write a story about the journey to this make-believe land. What was its name? What did the place look like? Who did she meet there? What happened?

Why: In this activity, the child's ability to use imagination is expanded and developed in depth.

When: This exercise can be done fairly regularly, perhaps once a month. It is probably too complex to do more frequently. It would be better to encourage an in-depth experience and allow plenty of time, rather than take a few minutes for a quick, superficial treatment. In fact, this exercise could take two or three journal sessions.

SIX

Fairy Tales and Stories

≪ ≪ ≪ ≪ ≪ ≫ ≫ ≫ ≫ ≫

Children are natural storytellers. They have an innate ability to create characters and develop plots and dialogue. By fostering this ability to play make-believe and to narrate and illustrate their world of imagination, we help children master language skills necessary for learning and communicating.

> I can recapture everything when I write, my thoughts, my ideals and my fantasies.
>
> I am the best and sharpest critic of my own work. I know myself what is and what is not well written. Anyone who doesn't write doesn't know how wonderful it is; I used to bemoan the fact that I couldn't draw at all, but now I am more than happy that I can at least write. And if I haven't any talent for writing books or newspaper articles, well then I can always write for myself.
>
> Anne Frank
> *Diary of a Young Girl*

≪ ≪ ≪ ≪ ≫ ≫ ≫ ≫

My Favorite Fairy Tale

How: Ask the child to think about his favorite fairy tale. If he can't think of one, mention the names of several ("Sleeping Beauty," "Jack-in-the-Beanstalk," "Snow White," "Tom Thumb," "The Princess and the Pea," "Goldilocks and the Three Bears," "Little Red Riding Hood"). Ask the child to draw a scene from his favorite fairy tale. If the child is older, he may want to draw a cartoon or comic strip of the story with balloons showing the dialogue.

When the drawing or cartoon is complete, suggest that the child write down his feelings about the story, the characters, and the events. Ask the child to write about any of his own experiences that are similar to events in the story. Has he ever felt like the hero of the story? If so, what happened to make him feel that way?

Why: This exercise helps the child to find universal themes in fairy tales through identification and empathy with the characters and their problems. In younger children it helps develop an understanding of sequence of events. For older children it illustrates the building of dramatic tension and resolution in a story.

When: This exercise need not be done repeatedly, but if it is repeated, a new fairy tale or story can be introduced and read aloud to provide variety and interest.

DOC
GRUMPY
SNEEZY
HAPPY
DOPEY
This is a picture of the fairy tale Snow-White and the Seven Dwarfs. The witch is giving Snow-White the poison apple.

≪ ≪ ≪ ≪ ≫ ≫ ≫ ≫

My Favorite Movie or Play

How: Ask the child to recall her favorite movie or play (or one she's seen recently that she liked). Ask the child to draw a picture of a scene from the movie or play or draw a cartoon comic strip of the story.

With an older youngster, suggest she write a review of the film or play after she's completed the drawing. Ask the child to write down why she liked the film or play and what personal meaning it had for her. Did she identify with any of the characters and, if so, who and why?

Why: This exercise encourages the child to observe all aspects of dramatic development and characterization and to see them as personally meaningful. It heightens an awareness of detail and sequence.

When: This activity can be done repeatedly, although it is probably better to do it less frequently but in depth. However, a child who is especially interested in film or drama may want to do it more often.

My Favorite Movie: Star Wars

Blasting lasers, strange inhuman creatures and non-stop planetary action, best describe my favorite movie. It is STAR WARS, a movie about a mission to save the rebel planet from the evil empire, and the clutches of the merciless Darth Vader. A beautiful princess, a young farm boy, and son of the Jedi Knight, a gambler, his funny apprentice and two mixed up robots are the main characters that together fight to save the planet. They run into strange creatures, fight enemy spaceships and are almost doomed everywhere they turn. But then they are allied with a wise old man who believes in the power of the *Force*. Star Wars is filled with danger, comedy, and suspense. I also thought the special effects were dazzling.

≪ ≪ ≪ ≪ ≫ ≫ ≫ ≫

My Favorite Television Show

How: Ask the child to think about his favorite television show, either a special or a series. Ask him to draw a picture of the main characters in the show.

Then suggest that the child let the characters give their names and tell about themselves. Encourage the child to imagine himself meeting these characters. What would he say to them, and what would they say to him? Ask the child to write all the dialogue down as if it were a script for a play.

Child: _____

Character: _____

Child: _____

Character: _____

Suggest that the child write his own original story using the characters in the television show. He can do it in the form of a storyboard, with pictures and captions, similar to a comic strip. Another option is to write a synopsis of the plot.

Why: In this exercise, the child is encouraged to build a dramatic story of his own using characters with unique personalities, motivations, and patterns of behavior. The child's choice of character is related to his psychological development and the parts of the child's personality that need expression.

When: This exercise can be done frequently. It is an excellent vehicle for exploring various personality types and is especially useful for children who are interested in or talented in drama, filmmaking, or video production.

≪ ≪ ≪ ≪ ≫ ≫ ≫ ≫
My Favorite Book

How: Suggest that the child think about her favorite book. Then suggest that she draw a scene from the book.

Ask the child to tell the story in her own words and illustrate it. Captions can accompany each picture. A younger child can do the exercise entirely in pictures with captions.

Encourage the child to write about why she liked the book and what she learned. This should include any personal experiences that helped her understand or appreciate the characters better.

WHY: This exercise helps children express their experiences of fictional characters and relate them to everyday life. It also expands drawing and writing abilities.

WHEN: This activity can be done frequently, especially when the child has read a book and expressed enthusiasm about it.

≪ ≪ ≪ ≪ ≫ ≫ ≫ ≫

My Favorite Character

How: Ask the child to think about his favorite character from a movie, play, television show, book, legend, or myth. Suggest that he draw a picture of the character.

Suggest that the child have an imaginary meeting with the character in which they talk to each other. Ask the child to write the conversation out like a play.

Child: _____

Character: _____

Child: _____

Character: _____

This is an interview in which the child can ask questions, tell the character how he feels about him or her, ask for advice, and so forth.

WHY: This exercise helps the child explore the human qualities and personality traits the character symbolizes. It increases his understanding of human nature.

WHEN: This exercise can be done fairly regularly and is especially useful when a child shows enthusiasm for a particular character. Children usually express such an interest through dramatic play, conversation, drawings, or displays of photographs of the character.

A Famous Person

How: Ask the child to think of a famous person she wishes she could meet. This person can be alive or dead, modern or historical, from any walk of life (entertainment, government, religion), and from any nation or culture.

Suggest that the child draw a picture of this famous person.

After the drawing is complete, suggest that the child have an imaginary conversation with this person. Ask the child to tell the person how she feels about him or her and why she feels that way. The child can ask questions, tell about herself, and carry on a conversation just as if the person were right there. Then suggest that the child write out the conversation like a play script.

Child: _____

Famous Person: _____

Child: _____

WHY: This exercise helps the child feel a rapport with people she usually thinks of as remote or unlike herself. By creating conversation, she can imagine actually being with this person as another human being like herself.

WHEN: This activity can be done regularly. It is perhaps most effective when the child already shows a genuine interest in some particular famous person.

≪ ≪ ≪ ≪ ≫ ≫ ≫ ≫

My Own Fairy Tale

How: Ask the child to create her own fairy tale. She is the central character (the heroine). The child invents characters, places, and situations; the other characters in the story can be fictional or based on real people. Suggest, however, that they be given fantasy names in keeping with the style of fairy tales.

Suggest that the child illustrate the original fairy tale.

Why: This exercise helps the child express inner challenges and use imagination to create new resolutions. It develops the ability to shape a dramatic plot and to create characters.

When: This activity need not be done repeatedly unless the vehicle is changed, for example, writing a television series or a short screenplay with the child as the main character.

≪ ≪ ≪ ≪ ≫ ≫ ≫ ≫

If I Were . . .

How: Ask the child to create a poem by completing the following sentence as many times as she wishes:
"If I were _____, I would _____."
   (person or animal)   (do)

Suggest that the child illustrate one or more of the sentences.

WHY: This exercise fosters imagination and poetic expression by encouraging a sense of whimsy and make-believe.

WHEN: This exercise can be done regularly, as often as once a week.

If I were ———, I would ———.

If I were *my mother,* I would look for the good instead of the bad.

If I were *the principal,* I would have more vacation and less school.

≪ ≪ ≪ ≪ ≫ ≫ ≫ ≫
Once Upon a Time

How: Ask the child to write a poem that begins with the line "Once upon a time . . ." Suggest that the poem rhyme. The poem can have meaning or be silly or nonsense.

WHY: This exercise encourages experimenting with language and advanced skills such as rhyming.

WHEN: This activity can be used on a regular basis. If used frequently, it is advisable to suggest other opening lines in order to provide variety and stimulate interest. The child (or children in the class) can be asked to provide new opening lines.

Once Upon a Time

Once upon a time it was my birthday,
My Mom, Dad and I went to see a play.

It was a Broadway play and that's fact,
It was "Annie." We went in and they started to act.

It had Annie, the orphans, the millionaire and secretary,
The criminals, the President (FDR) and, oh, so many!

So all through the play I had a jolly time.
By the way, my birthday was for my turning nine!

≪ ≪ ≪ ≪ ≫ ≫ ≫ ≫

The Monsters and Me

How: Ask the child to draw a picture of herself and the monster in her life. They may be monsters that appear in dreams, imaginary monsters, or people who appear to be like monsters because the child is afraid of them. Suggest that the child show how she deals with these monsters.

Ask the child to talk to the monster, asking what it wants from her, what it wants to give or teach her. Then she tells it what she wants. She then writes this down.

Why: All children have fantasy monsters of one kind or another. This exercise helps them confront their monsters and handle their fear instead of being victimized. Once the monsters are out in the open they are not as frightening.

When: This exercise can be done periodically, but it is especially useful when a child is having nightmares about monsters or shows a fear of monsters in conversation or other behavior.

"This is a picture of half ME *and half werewolf."*

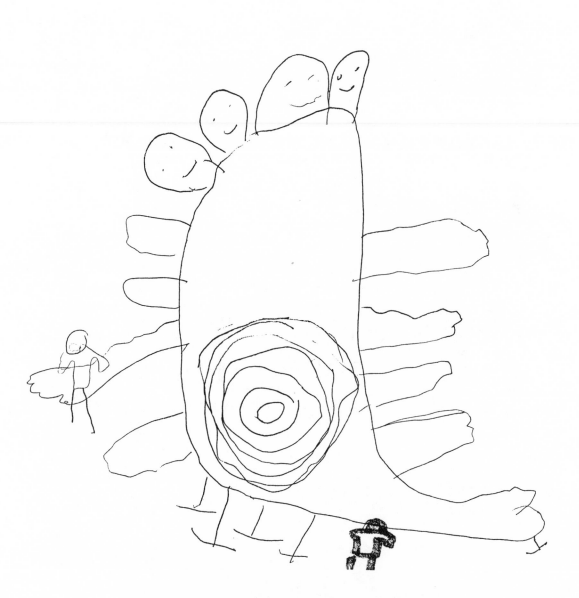

"This is a monster with 4 heads and 4 feet and 8 arms. The monster grabbed a little boy. Another little boy is waiting. I don't want to talk to this monster. He smells too much!!!"

Monster

This is the Monster Eye in the sky. He's a mean monster. I am on the ground and I am zapping him with a laser.

≪ ≪ ≪ ≪ ≫ ≫ ≫ ≫

Scary Fairy Tale

How: Suggest that the child write out a scary fairy tale with a happy ending.

Ask the child to illustrate the happy ending.

WHY: This is an extension of "The Monsters and Me" exercise. It enables the child to develop frightening situations and resolve them through creative problem solving. The ability to solve problems creatively can be applied in everyday life.

WHEN: This exercise is a good follow-up to "The Monsters and Me" and is effective for use with children who are troubled with nightmares.

≪ ≪ ≪ ≪ ≫ ≫ ≫ ≫

Show and Tell: My Own Cartoon

How: Suggest that the child create his own comic strip by inventing characters, a setting, and a story and drawing the story in a series of "frames" with balloons and captions. The first time it can be done with a few frames. Later on the child can create longer stories and do them in ten or more frames.

Why: This exercise helps children learn to visualize as they tell a story. It develops their sensitivity to dramatic development, story or plot building, and characterization.

When: This exercise can be done regularly. It can be combined with any exercise in which a story is being told and is especially appropriate for young children who can't write very well or at all.

SEVEN

Dreams and Wishes

≪ ≪ ≪ ≪ ≪ ≫ ≫ ≫ ≫ ≫

I am young and I possess many buried qualities; I am
young and strong and am living a great adventure. . . .
Every day I feel that I am developing inward . . .

Dear Kitty,
The sun is shining, the sky is a deep blue, there is a lovely
breeze and I'm longing—so longing—for everything. To
talk, for freedom, for friends, to be alone. And I do so
long . . . to cry! I feel as if I'm going to burst, and I know
that it would get better with crying; but I can't, I'm restless,
I go from one room to the other, breathe through the crack
of a closed window, feel my heart beating, as if it is saying,
"Can't you satisfy my longings at last?"

I believe that it is spring within me, I feel that spring is
awakening, I feel it in my whole body and soul. It is an
effort to behave normally, I feel utterly confused, don't
know what to read, what to write, what to do, I only know
that I am longing . . . !

> Yours, Anne

Who would ever think that so much can go on in the soul
of a young girl?

I hope that I have acquired a bit of insight and will use it
well when the occasion arises.

> Anne Frank
> *Diary of a Young Girl*

≪ ≪ ≪ ≪ ≫ ≫ ≫ ≫

Draw a Dream

How: Ask the child to recall a dream and to draw a picture of any part or all of the dream. If it was a long dream, she may need to draw more than one picture. If she only remembers a part of the dream (an image or a scene), suggest that she draw that.

After the child has drawn whatever she can remember, suggest that she write down whatever thoughts come into her head in "free association" to the images in the picture.

Why: Dreams are powerful messages from the unconscious. Often children have frightening or disturbing dreams. This exercise can help them handle the emotions and issues coming from the unconscious through dreams.

When: This exercise can be done whenever the child has a recurring or powerful dream that had evoked strong emotions or left an indelible imprint on the memory. It is an excellent way for young children who cannot write to deal with dreams.

"I dreamt of a roller coaster without wheels. No tracks. Just plain drifting. It was fun—not scary."

≪ ≪ ≪ ≪ ≫ ≫ ≫ ≫

Tell a Dream

How: Suggest that the child write down a dream he has had, describing what happened in the present tense, as if the dream were happening now. Suggest that he leave spaces between the lines.

After he writes the dream out, ask the child to change to a contrasting color pen. In the spaces beneath each line, the child can now write down anything that comes to mind that relates the dream narrative to everyday life.

Why: As with the previous exercise, "Draw a Dream," this is a tool for remembering and understanding dreams. It provides good practice in narrative writing. It also sharpens the child's sensitivity to symbols and metaphors.

When: This exercise can be done in combination with "Draw a Dream" or done alone.

A Dream

I am flying on a plane, bound for California, to see my father. I will finally be getting there, after waiting a whole year. Then suddenly the plane shoots downward towards the mountains. I feel a violent jolt, the plane has crashed. I look around and I am the only one alive. I have many broken bones, but I manage to crawl through the bloody bodies, and out the emergency door. Just as I get out, it blows up. I wait and wait, then a helicopter comes! My father is even in it. I am safe.*

(*I think I had this dream because every time something good is going, fate has to get me, then it turns bad. I survived the crash, because I'm a survivor. I've been through a lot in my life. You notice just my Dad came to rescue me because he *really* cares about me, more than others. Since I had this dream I'm kinda scared to fly in a plane. I know I'll be nervous flying to my Dad's this summer.)

≪ ≪ ≪ ≪ ≫ ≫ ≫ ≫

Feel a Dream

How: Ask the child to remember a dream. She can draw it or write it out if she wishes, but this is not necessary. Then suggest that she let each part of the dream (i.e., each person, animal, or object) talk in the first person and the present tense. Ask her to write this dialogue out like a play script.

bowl: I am the blue bowl. I'm fragile. You have to be careful with me. I break when you drop me.

sister: I saw you drop the bowl. I think you were careless and that mother will be angry when she finds out.

me: I dropped the bowl by accident and I got scared when my sister saw it happen. I'm afraid my mother will get mad and punish me.

Why: This is a way for the dreamer to experience the thoughts and feelings contained in each symbol image in her dream. It is also good practice in examining motivation and cause and effect in events and relationships.

When: This approach to understanding the hidden meaning of a dream can be used alone or in combination with the two preceding exercises.

≪ ≪ ≪ ≪ ≫ ≫ ≫ ≫

Dream Story

How: Suggest that the child write out a dream that he recalls. If the dream had an unhappy ending or it was interrupted and the child felt unresolved, suggest that he write an ending he likes. For instance, in the example for the "Feel a Dream" exercise, the dream ended on a note of fear. The child could finish the dream with mother coming home and finding the bowl was broken but *not* being upset about it and telling the child that there is nothing to fear.

WHY: This is an important technique because it helps the child to have some creative control over events in his dreams. After all, the dream belongs to the child, so he can do whatever he wants with it. It helps the child feel powerful in the face of mysterious and often upsetting messages from dreams.

WHEN: This is an especially useful exercise for a child who has a troubling dream or recurring nightmares. In fact, before going to sleep the child can suggest to himself that if scary things happen in his dream, he will deal with the situation and come out of it triumphant.

≪ ≪ ≪ ≪ ≫ ≫ ≫ ≫

I Wish

How: Ask the child to imagine that he is being granted a wish. What would it be? Ask him to draw a picture of it.

Suggest that the child write a poem entitled "I wish . . ." It need not rhyme. Encourage the child to simply let the words flow out. The poem does not have to be about the picture, but it can be if the child wants to connect them.

WHY: This exercise develops imagination and poetic expression and fosters a sense of self.

WHEN: This activity can be done at regular intervals, perhaps monthly.

I Wish

I wish I could say goodbye,
to sorrow and despair,
shake off all the loneliness,
when my heart's about to tear.

I wish I had a world,
that overflowed with love,
a place filled with happiness,
where the sun always shone above.

I wish I had a Mom and Dad,
together in one house they filled,
who laughed and cried with me,
and all my dreams helped build.

I wish I had a puppy,
cute and cuddly I'd prefer,
who brushed my face when I came near,
with his silky soft fur.

≪ ≪ ≪ ≪ ≫ ≫ ≫ ≫

If I Had Three Wishes

How: Suggest that the child make up a story in which she encounters a character, real or fictitious, who grants her three wishes. Ask her to describe how and where she met the character, what the character said, and what the wishes were. Suggest that she include a description of the effects of the fulfilled wishes. How did it change her life? Encourage the child to elaborate.

Why: This is an excellent tool for developing imagination, storytelling skills, and a sense of consequences from decisions and actions.

When: This activity can be done more than once but not necessarily on a regular basis.

Here are my three wishes . . .

1. That there would be no destruction like fires, tornados, hurricanes, earthquakes, etc.
2. That my family and I would be millionaires ($!)
3. That anything I ever wished for would come true.

≪ ≪ ≪ ≪ ≫ ≫ ≫ ≫

Three Magic Doors

How: Ask the child to close her eyes and pretend she is standing in front of three closed doors. Have the child imagine where the doors are, what kind of building they are in, what kind of doors they are (their color, material, design).

Have the child open her eyes and suggest that she draw the three doors, including any signs or symbols she may have seen on them. Explain that behind each door there is (1) an opportunity, (2) a challenge, and (3) a helper (in that order). Use whatever terms the child understands to convey the idea, or simply say that there are three surprises behind the doors.

After the drawing of the doors is completed, suggest that the child draw another picture. This time she portrays what is behind the three doors. It can be a three-part picture or three separate pictures.

After drawing the pictures, the child can write about what she found behind the doors.

Why: In this exercise, the child is exploring her values in greater detail. She is letting her unconscious wishes rise to the surface of her conscious mind.

When: This exercise need not be done often, once every few weeks or so is usually adequate. It is very helpful for children and teens who have difficulty being motivated or finding activities and interests they enjoy.

Music, lots of records and instruments!

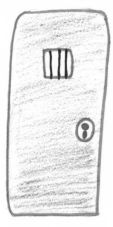

Darkness, emptiness, and loneliness.

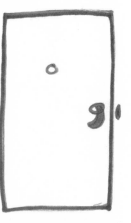

Beautiful flowers and plants, running rivers. Paradise.

≪ ≪ ≪ ≪ ≫ ≫ ≫ ≫

My Dream House

How: Suggest that the child close his eyes and imagine that he can build his dream house. It can be anywhere he likes and can be whatever he wants. Let him sit quietly and picture it in his mind. Then ask him to draw a floor plan of his dream house. He can label the rooms or areas and show areas around the house if he wishes.

Ask the child to write about his floor plan and about what he pictured in his mind while visualizing his dream house. Where is it? What kind of place is it? What would he do there? Who would be there with him, or would he be alone?

Then suggest that the child write down how his imaginary dream house reflects his personality.

Why: This exercise is excellent training in creative visualization, which provides images and details for descriptive writing.

When: This activity can be done repeatedly but should be varied by introducing other themes such as a trip to outer space, a visit to another planet, a journey to a foreign country.

My Dream House

Looking from a distance, you would see a two story, stone house, with ivy growing up and down the front. As you walk in, it would be very sunny, because of all the numerous windows. There are plenty of rooms, enough for all my books and instruments, and a big kitchen, so you wouldn't bump into people. There are enough telephones and baths to go around too. It is all done in antiques, and plants bloom everywhere. To make it energy efficient, solar panels and fireplaces are my heat. I have a pool, greenhouse and gym. Everything I always wanted and more.

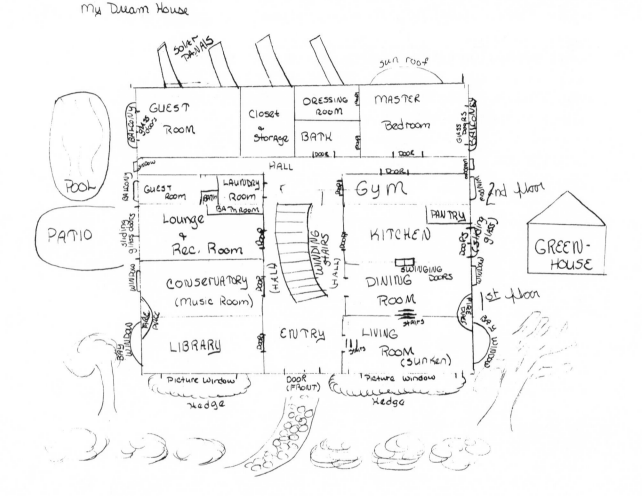

My Dream House

≪ ≪ ≪ ≪ ≫ ≫ ≫ ≫

Dreams of Glory

How: Ask the child to think about something special she'd like to accomplish or experience or do. Suggest that she close her eyes and visualize the event in detail.

Then ask the child to write about it in the past tense, *as if it has already happened.* Encourage her to describe it in detail. Where was she, what happened, and how did she feel about it?

WHY: This exercise develops imagination and the ability to make dreams come true through visualization and positive thinking. As in the preceding exercise, "My Dream House," it helps the child write descriptive prose from mental imagery.

WHEN: This activity can be done on a regular basis and can be expanded by doing the next exercise, "In My Life."

≪ ≪ ≪ ≪ ≫ ≫ ≫ ≫

In My Life

How: Ask the child to make a list of all the things she'd like to do or accomplish in her lifetime. Encourage her to let her imagination fly and to include her wildest dreams even if she thinks they're not possible or practical.

WHY: We often limit ouselves by thinking of our fondest dreams and aspirations as impractical. We then deny ourselves the development of our creative talents and true potential. This exercise and the one preceding it, "Dreams of Glory," encourage the child to express her dreams; it can be the first step toward realizing them.

WHEN: This exercise can be done regularly, by adding to the list. It is another important tool for clarifying values and goals and strengthening a sense of self and personal desires.

≪ ≪ ≪ ≪ ≫ ≫ ≫ ≫

Treasure Map

How: Ask the child to close his eyes and picture his "buried treasure." Explain that this buried treasure is a talent or ability he has within him.

Suggest that the child open his eyes and draw a map showing the path leading to his buried treasure. The buried treasure should be included in the drawing. On the path there are obstacles as well as helpers, which should be drawn and labeled.

After the map is completed, ask the child to talk with the obstacles and the helpers and to write down what was said. This can be written as the script for a play or as a cartoon with word balloons. Whichever form is used, the child finally gets to the buried treasure.

WHY: Through the use of imagination, the child is exploring his own hidden potential as well as his power to confront and overcome obstacles and achieve his goals. This is an excellent tool for values clarification.

WHEN: This exercise can be done repeatedly and can be varied by asking the child to choose new goals, abilities, or experiences symbolized by the "buried treasure" image.

≪ ≪ ≪ ≪ ≫ ≫ ≫ ≫

When I Grow Up

How: Share the following quote from Langston Hughes: "Hold fast to dreams, for if dreams die, life is a broken winged bird that cannot fly."*

Ask the child to think about all the things he's thought he'd like to be when he grows up. He can go back in his memory to the first time he thought about it. Suggest that he make a list of all his fantasies about what he'd like to be when he grows up. The list should start with his earliest wishes, no matter how impractical or whimsical. For instance, sometimes very young children want to be Mickey Mouse or Superman or an animal when they grow up. Then ask the child to continue the list up to and including his current wishes.

After the list is complete, suggest that the child select his favorite item, the one that seems most enjoyable. Ask him to draw himself as that item on the list.

When the drawing is complete, suggest that he let the character "speak" by writing down what he would say if he could talk. Let the pictured "character" introduce himself by name, tell about himself, what he does, and how he feels.

WHY: This exercise encourages the child to explore options, develop personal values and desires, and give full expression to his dreams and wishes.

WHEN: This activity can be done regularly by adding to the list, selecting new "favorites" from the list, and writing them out as suggested above.

*The Langston Hughes quote can be used to introduce any of the exercises in this chapter that explore fantasies and wishes.